Curricular Perspectives on Teaching English as a Foreign Language in the World

Nihal Yurtseven (ed.)

Curricular Perspectives on Teaching English as a Foreign Language in the World

PETER LANG

**Bibliographic Information published by the
Deutsche Nationalbibliothek**
The Deutsche Nationalbibliothek lists this publication in the Deutsche
Nationalbibliografie; detailed bibliographic data is available online at
http://dnb.d-nb.de.

Library of Congress Cataloging-in-Publication Data
A CIP catalog record for this book has been applied for at the
Library of Congress.

Cover illustration:
© New Africa Studio / shutterstock.com

Funded by Bahçeşehir University

ISBN 978-3-631-87570-4 (Print)
E-ISBN 978-3-631-88803-2 (E-PDF)
E-ISBN 978-3-631-88804-9 (E-PUB)
10.3726/b20324

© Peter Lang GmbH
Internationaler Verlag der Wissenschaften
Berlin 2022
All rights reserved.

Peter Lang – Berlin · Bruxelles · Istanbul · Lausanne · New York · Oxford

This publication has been peer reviewed.

www.peterlang.com

Table of Contents

Foreword

This book has been prepared to help researchers who are interested in gaining a multi-dimensional perspective on different approaches to teaching English as a foreign language (EFL) in the world. As we all know, curricular decisions are shaped under the influence of societal, economic, political, philosophical, and several other factors. As such, each country goes through a different process, and this can make considerable differences in the integration of EFL approaches to education systems. This book tries to show how different countries handle the situation by depicting both the overall education system and EFL teaching approaches in each chapter. The content of the book will help the readers gain perspective about making a comparative analysis of how English is taught in the world.

Curricular Perspectives on Teaching English as a Foreign Language in the World is organized into 10 chapters. Turkey, Finland, France, Germany, Singapore, Slovakia, Estonia, Mexico, Ecuador, and Israel are examined in consecutive chapters about their education system and their EFL curriculum. Each chapter provides some traces of the history and experiences of the examined country and gives signals about the underlying reasons for and the rationale behind the current implementations. In short, we try to provide readers with a multifaceted perspective on how English is taught in the world with the addition of some background information.

Acknowledgments

I wish to express my deep appreciation to all the authors, who showed continuous dedication and interest in the publication of this book from the beginning. I feel grateful to them as they gracefully and patiently handled my numerous modification requests. I would like to thank Prof. Dr. Tunç Bozbura, the Vice president of Bahçeşehir University for his great encouragement and enthusiasm in preparing this publication. Lastly, I would like to thank Prof. Dr. Şirin Karadeniz, the President of Bahçeşehir University for her continued guidance and support and the peaceful environment she created to concentrate on completing this endeavor.

Assoc. Prof. Dr. Nihal Yurtseven
Bahçeşehir University, Istanbul, Turkey
July, 2022

Sezgin Ballıdağ

Turkey: An Insight into the Language Curriculum

Lecturer, School of Foreign Languages, Yildiz Technical University, Istanbul,
Turkey
PhD student, English Language Education, Bahcesehir University, Istanbul,
Turkey
sballidag@gmail.com / sezgin.ballidag@bahcesehir.edu.tr

Abstract

The education systems of countries have been evolving depending on the needs of learners, and governments are doing their best to increase the quality of their education to compete with the competitive international labour market. Due to the growing need for competent language speakers in international business, teaching, and learning, English has become a vital component in the curriculum of countries. Turkey is one of those countries which highlights the importance of English education as a key to social, economic, and social progress of the nation. This study provides an insight into the new English language curriculum of the Ministry of National Education (MoNE) in Turkey, by developing an understanding of the way English is taught at primary and various secondary school types in Turkey together with the philosophical underpinnings of foreign language education in the country.

Keywords: MoNE, language education, foreign language curriculum, Turkey

Introduction

Turkey changed its education system in the 2012–2013 education year and legislated 12-year mandatory (4+4+4) education. In this change, the place of foreign language education was as significant as any other school subject since to be able to communicate effectively in the global arena and progress economically as well as socially depends heavily on the ability to speak English. This sudden change mandated an immediate need for redesigning the curricula including English instruction. In the new education system, English instruction was mandated from 2nd grade and onward, making the onset of language learning 2 years earlier. In the new curricula, principles of the Common European Framework of Reference for Languages: Learning, Teaching, Assessment (CEFR) have been adopted. As CEFR puts a special emphasis on transferring students' knowledge of real-life practices to support fluency, proficiency, and retention of the language (CoE, 2001), the use of the language in authentic, real-life contexts in the new English curriculum has been highlighted. In line with the tenets of CEFR, there is also a strong emphasis in the new curriculum on the use of English as a way of communication rather than seeing it as an end product.

The use of language for communication as the *communicative approach* entails real authentic use of the language in the contexts where there is interaction between the interlocuters (Larsen-Freeman & Anderson, 2011). Due to the importance attached to the genuineness of the interaction between peers and their interaction with the teacher, classroom materials are chosen from authentic sources.

Another important aspect of the new curriculum is the focus it attaches to the values education. The key values in the curriculum include justice, friendship, self-control, honesty, patience, respect, love, responsibility, patriotism, and altruism. These values are embedded in the topics and themes of the syllabi (Primary Education English Teaching Program, 2018).

The Structure of the Curriculum in Primary Education

At the primary education level, the curriculum is divided into three main stages: grades 2–4, 5–6, and 7–8. As can be seen in Figure 1, the skill focus and main activities/strategies are clearly identified in the curriculum. Since children learn best through games, songs, or hands-on exercise (Cameron, 2001), in the first stage (2–4), the focus is mainly on listening and speaking with very limited exercise on grammar and reading. As the learners advance in language skills in grades 5–6, they start to be exposed to short texts and are required to do controlled writing activities such as filling out a form with their personal information. Finally in grades 7 and 8, a more integrated approach is adopted where students both read simple texts and write simple stories. There is a progression from cognitively undemanding activities towards cognitively demanding tasks.

Levels [CEFR*] (Hours / Week)	Grades	Skill focus	Main activities/Strategies
1 [A1] (2)	2	Listening and Speaking	TPR/Arts and crafts/Drama
	3	Listening and Speaking Very Limited Reading and Writing°	
	4	Listening and Speaking Very Limited Reading and Writing°	
2 [A1] (3)	5	Listening and Speaking Limited Reading° Very Limited Writing°	Drama/Role-play
	6	Listening and Speaking Limited Reading° Limited Writing°	
3 [A2] (4)	7	**Primary:** Listening and Speaking **Secondary:** Reading and Writing	Theme-based ∞
	8	**Primary:** Listening and Speaking **Secondary:** Reading and Writing	

Figure 1 Model English Language Curriculum (for 2nd–8th Grades)

According to the latest change that will be implemented as of the 2022–2023 education year, the number of English lessons taught at elementary and middle schools can be seen in Table 1.

Table 1 The Number of English Lesson Hours (Grades 2–8)

	Grades						
	2	3	4	5	6	7	8
Compulsory	2	2	2	3	3	4	4
Selective				2	2	2	2

As the table shows, the number of English lessons increases as students progress towards grade 8, and from grade 5 and onwards (middle school), they can take 2 hours of elective English courses.

Instructional Materials

For each level, there are 10 units that evolve around various themes. The units are organized in themes, which is also supported by Hale and Cunningham (2011) as it is easier to present new information in a relevant manner. The curriculum provides a suggested lesson plan for each unit at each level. As can be seen in

Figure 2, there are three columns for functions and useful language, language skills and outcomes, and suggested contexts, tasks, and assignments. Teachers and program developers are recommended not to skip any item in the plan since they are presented in a cyclical manner, that is, skipping on function or task may result in difficulty to grasp a linguistic item in the following tasks.

Unit / Theme	Functions & Useful Language	Language Skills and Learning Outcomes	Suggested Contexts, Tasks and Assignments
10 Nature	**Expressing likes and dislikes** I like/love dolphins, but I dislike sharks. **Making simple inquiries** Are there four dolphins? — Yes, there are four dolphins. — No. There is one dolphin. — There are four dolphins/ trees in the sea/forest **Talking about nature and animals** This/That/It is a frog. It's big and green. Is the whale red? — Yes, it is. — No, it isn't. — This whale/It is blue. bee, -s bear, -s dolphin,-s forest, -s frog, -s ladybird,-s mountain, -s pigeon, -s sea shark, -s whale, -s	**Listening** **E3.10.L1.** Students will be able to recognize nature and the names of animals. **E3.10.L2.** Students will be able to follow short and simple oral instructions about nature and animals. **Speaking** **E3.10.S1.** Students will be able to talk about nature and animals. **E3.10.S2.** Students will be able to talk about the animals they like or dislike and the nature.	**Contexts** Advertisements Blogs Captions Cartoons Conversations Illustrations Maps Signs Songs Stories Tables Videos **Tasks/Activities** Arts and Crafts Chants and Songs Drama (Role Play, Simulation, Pantomime) Drawing and Coloring Games Labeling Matching Making Puppets Questions and Answers Reordering **Assignments** • Students complete and reflect on their visual dictionaries. • In groups, students prepare animal masks and color them.

Figure 2 3rd Grade Unit 10 Suggested Plan

Besides adopting a communicative approach to language teaching, developing *intercultural competencies* is another concern of the language syllabus of the country. For Byram (2000) intercultural communicative competence (ICC) is the ability to be able to interact in an effective way with people from different cultures. Intercultural competence is also defined as "a complex of abilities needed to perform effectively and appropriately when interacting with others who are linguistically and culturally different from oneself" (Fantini, 2006, p. 12). To this end, elements from various cultures are integrated into the syllabus to help students appreciate other cultures while valuing their own. An example of how to integrate different cultures into the curriculum can be seen in Figure 3.

As shown in Figure 3, this part of the book aims to familiarize students with the breakfast habits of different nations such as Britain and Spain. As stated in the goals of the curriculum, students also appreciate their own culture by having a chance to talk about it with their peers.

A. Read the text and write True (T) or False (F) .
Then correct the False statements.

Mr. Hunter: Good morning, everybody! Welcome to "It's Breakfast Time" on Chefs' Channel. Today, we are talking about the breakfast habits of different countries. We have some guests.
Here we have a chef from the UK., Mr. Cook.
Hi, Mr. Cook. What do the British people have for breakfast?

Mr. Cook: Hi, Mr. Hunter. In Britain, we have eggs, sausages, mushrooms and baked beans for breakfast. We also like tea with milk at breakfast.

Mr. Hunter: Thank you, Mr. Cook. Now, it's time to see what Spanish people have for breakfast. Mrs. Cocinero is giving information about the traditional Spanish breakfast.

Mrs. Cocinero: Spanish people have toast and fruit juice for breakfast. We have different kinds of toasts.

Mr. Hunter: Thank you, Mrs. Cocinero.What about you, Mr. Aşçı?
Can you talk about breakfast habits of Turkish people?

Mr. Aşçı: We have olives, cheese, eggs, tomatoes, butter and honey in Turkey.

Mr. Cook: It sounds yummy!
Mr. Hunter: Thanks for joining our programme.

Figure 3 6th Grade English Book Example

Testing and Assessment

In line with the CFR, various forms of alternative and process-oriented assessment techniques are suggested in the English curriculum. Those techniques include portfolio assessment, project assessment, creative drama tasks, etc. Besides alternative assessments, students also take written and oral exams, quizzes, and homework assignments during the semester. In the curriculum, both summative and formative tools are mentioned as important sources of assessing students' knowledge. Although with the new language curriculum, the onset of language instruction became 2nd grade, no summative testing was administered in 2nd and 3rd grades to arouse positive attitudes and beliefs towards language learning. According to the regulation, from the 4th until the 8th, students have two written exams for each semester. Figure 4 displays the testing techniques and suggestions for test preparation.

Language Skills	Testing Techniques*	Suggestions for Test Preparation
Speaking	Collaborative or singular drama performances (Simulations, Role-plays, Side-coaching), Debates, Group or pair discussions, Describing a picture/video/story, etc., Discussing a picture/video/story, etc., Giving short responses in specific situations, Information gap, Opinion gap, Reporting an event/anecdote, etc., Short presentations, Talking about a visual/table/chart, etc.	• Make sure you have prepared a reliable assessment rubric to assess students. • Anxiety and inhibition may cause problems: Provide a relaxing atmosphere in testing. • Encourage self- and peer-assessment if applies (for higher proficiency grades).
Listening	Different variations of matching (... the sentences with paragraphs ... pictures with the sentences, etc.), Discriminating between phonemes, Identifying interlocutors' intentions and implicatures, Listen and perform/complete an action (E.g.: Listen and draw/paint, listen and match, listen and put the correct order, listen and spot the mistake, etc.), Listen and tick (the words, the themes, the situations or events, the people, etc.), Omitting the irrelevant information, Putting into order/reordering, Recognizing phonemic variations, Selective listening for morphological structure and affixation, True/False/No information, Understanding overall meaning and supporting details, Recognizing specific information, Questions and answers.	• Include both bottom-up and top-down listening techniques. •Bottom-up techniques typically focus on sounds, words, intonation, important grammatical structures, and other components of spoken language. • Top-down techniques are concerned with the activation of schemata, with deriving meaning, with global understanding, and with the interpretation of a text.
Reading	Different variations of matching (... the sentences with paragraphs, ... pictures with the sentences, etc.), Finding specific information, Finding a title to a text, Identifying the gist and supporting details, Intensive reading, Read and perform / complete and action (E.g.: Read and guess the meaning of lexemes, Read and draw/paint, Read and solve the riddle), Solving a puzzle, Spotting text mechanics (reference, substitution, various types ellipses), True/False/No information, Transferring the text to a table/chart (Information transfer), Understanding the author's intention, Questions and answers.	• Include both bottom-up and top-down reading techniques. •Bottom-up techniques focus on morphological dynamics, words, collocations, key grammatical structures, and other components of written language. • Top-down techniques are concerned with the activation of schemata, with deriving meaning, with global understanding, and with the interpretation of a text.
Writing	Describing a picture/visual/video, etc., Filling in a form (hotel check in form, job application form, etc.), Note taking/making, Preparing an outline, Preparing a list (shopping list, a to-do list, etc.), Reporting a table or a chart, Rephrasing, Rewriting, Writing short notes, entries and responses, Writing a paragraph/e-mail/journal entry/etc., Writing a topic sentence/thesis statement	• Make sure you have prepared a reliable assessment rubric to assess students. • Provide a Genre (what to write), Audience (whom to write) and Purpose (why to write) for each writing assessment task. • Encourage self- and peer-assessment if applies (for higher proficiency grades).
Samples for Integrated Skills	Summarizing a text (listening/reading and writing), Taking notes (listening and writing), Reporting an event (listening/reading and speaking), Paraphrasing (listening/reading and writing), Preparing a mind-map (reading/listening and writing), Cloze/C-test (reading and writing), Dictation (listening and writing), Read a text and present it (reading and speaking), Write a text and present it (writing and speaking), Outlining a reading text (reading and writing)	• Offer authentic or real-like tasks to promote communicative testing. • Avoid offering tasks beyond students' current intellectual and cognitive maturity. • Provide samples to trigger task completion via linguistic performance.
Alternative Assessment	Portfolio Assessment, Project Assessment, Performance Assessment, Creative Drama Tasks, Class Newspaper/Social Media Projects, Journal Performance, etc.	• Determine initially the content, criteria for task inclusion, describe criteria for grading and the analytic rubric carefully, and present those aspects to the students before the application. Make sure students understand and accept the rules of application. • Encourage the inclusion of all language skills in portfolio content with equal weight and value. • Note that portfolio assessment procedure would be incomplete and thus useless without feedback and reflection.

* Please note that the testing techniques offered in the table are merely suggestions; different testing techniques that comply with the communicative testing philosophy may be exploited by the teachers, course book authors and material developers.

Figure 4 Suggested Testing Techniques and Suggestions for Test Preparation

Secondary Education

The curriculum for secondary education is also designed in line with the principles of CEFR, hence, students' proficiency levels are articulated as A1, A2, B1, and B1 levels. The number of English lessons per week depends on the types of high schools. Table 2 displays the number of English lessons that students at various high schools in Turkey have.

Table 2 The Number of English Lessons at High Schools

School Types	Preparatory Class	Grade 9	Grade 10	Grade 11	Grade 12
Anatolian High Schools		4	4	4	4
Anatolian High Schools with Preparatory Class	20	4	4	4	4
Social Sciences High School	20	4	4	2	2
Science High School		4	4	4	4
Fine Arts High School		2	2	2	2
Sports High School		2	2	2	2

School Types	Prepara-tory Class	Grade 9	Grade 10	Grade 11	Grade 12
Imam-Hatip High School with Pre-paratory Class	20	5	2	2	2
Vocational and Tech-nical High School		5	2	2	2

As shown in Table 2, the number of English lessons varies from 2 to 20 depending on the school type. While at Social Sciences high schools, religious vocational high schools with preparatory class and vocational technical high schools the number of English lessons decreases towards grade 12, at other school types, students take the same number of English lessons throughout their high school years.

The goal of the new English curriculum is defined as follows:

> The main goal of the new 9th-12th grades English Curriculum is to engage learners of English in stimulating, motivating, and enjoyable learning environments so that they become effective, fluent, and self-directed users of English. (Secondary Education English Teaching Program, 2018)

As can be seen from the quotation, fluent and self-directed speakers of the English language are among the major goals of the curriculum, and to achieve that goal, strong collaboration among all the stakeholders is suggested.

The curriculum of 9th–12th grades is seen as a continuance of the curriculum of 2nd–8th grade. Students start high school with a revision of A1 level and then proceed until B2 level in the last grade (Figure 5).

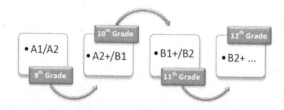

Figure 5 CEFR Levels According to the Grades

One principle behind the new language curriculum is that English is seen as a lingua franca and international language in the global world; therefore, students need it "to cross the borders literally and figuratively (McKay, 2002, p. 81).

It is an acknowledged fact that many learners of English in Turkey lack communicative competence since too much importance is attached to grammatical knowledge (Secondary Education English Teaching Program, 2018). Hence, to overcome this problem, the new 9th–12th-grade curriculum addresses the four skills and functions of the language to raise the communicative competence of the learners.

Testing and Assessment

A blend of traditional, alternative, and digital assessment tools is suggested in the language curriculum of 9th–12th grades. The main suggested assessment types are using discussion or video blogs to evaluate listening/speaking, Tech-Pack to evaluate four skills through exercies in listening, speaking reading and writing. There are also classical pen and paper exams, and e- portfolios. Figure 6 represents an example page that depicts a page with a video blog and e- portfolio entry. Being one of the alternative assessment methods, e-portfolios are pre-ferred as they can expand the array of materials that can be utilized (Walker & White, 2013).

E-PORTFOLIO ENTRY

A. Read the information below.

+ You should have an individual blog.
+ You can use your blog as an e-portfolio and keep your project work for each unit in it.
+ You should keep your e-portfolio under the supervision of your teacher.
+ You should also submit all the projects to your teacher at the end of this term.

B. Read the instructions below and do the project.

+ Ask your family members questions about their favorite free time activities.
+ Prepare a poster about their answers. You can make the poster online.
+ Hand in your project next week.
+ When your teacher gives it back, don't forget to take a photo of your project and upload it to your blog.

 VIDEO BLOG ENTRY

A. Read the paragraph below and learn what a video blog entry is.

What is a video blog entry?
It is a short video clip. You can prepare a video blog entry (vlog) in the classroom as part of pair work or group work activities. Or you can do it at home as a homework assignment. When you record your vlogs, you can use a digital camcorder, a laptop, a tablet or a smartphone. Your teacher should check your recordings before you share them in class. Your friends can fill in peer evaluation checklists after they watch the vlogs so they can evaluate your fluency and accuracy in English.

B. Work in pairs. Read the instructions below and prepare your video blog entry.

+ Write ten questions about everyday life and prepare a questionnaire together.
+ One of you is the interviewer and asks the questions.
+ Ask and answer with the correct intonation.
+ Record your conversation.
+ Upload your video blog entry by the end of this weekend. Share it on your blog.
+ Your partner and you will fill in the peer evaluation checklists for each other after watching the video.

Figure 6 An example of an E-Portfolio and Video Blog Entry from Grade 10 Coursebook

The Use of Technology and Blended Learning

Rapidly developing technologies enabled English language teaching to be more effective since these developments allow learners to progress in their own time and when necessary (Sung et al., 2016). With the ease technology brings with itself, for the last decades, there has been a great focus on Information and Communication Technologies (ICT) as they support language learning in numerous ways to enrich language and vocabulary development (Constantinescu, 2007). Learning environments that utilize technology may create autonomous learners (Chen et al., 2019). Besides creating autonomy in the classroom, teachers can also benefit from ICT to create variety in the classroom (Looi et al., 2020). The activities that can be done in the classroom are boundless, so when learner autonomy is combined with limitless online tools, student involvement increases, which leads to a concomitant rise in language development. Chanier and Selva (1998) favor using technology in the classroom claiming that Computer Assisted Language Learning (CALL) is fruitful, especially with vocabulary development.

Due to all the benefits of technology in the language classroom, the English curriculum for 9th–12th grades promotes blended learning, which combines face-to-face lessons with online lessons. To be able to use blended learning efficiently, explicit teaching is required to make the learners aware of the ways they can communicate online (Biesenbach-Lucas, 2007). Having trained in using online materials, teachers and students are able to benefit from online sources such as Tech Pack, an online environment where teachers can share supplementary materials, e-portfolios, or video blogs. These sources are of great help to supplement classroom learning in a blended way.

In order to increase the awareness of adolescents in technology use in English classes, some themes in the coursebooks include topics like netiquette or implications of technology. The new curriculum seeks to raise the technological knowledge of the individuals both by making them read about technology and use the technology themselves. To this end, some of the materials are also offered with multimedia as well as in print. In the curriculum, various materials (both print and multimedia) are suggested to the teachers, which are displayed in Figure 7.

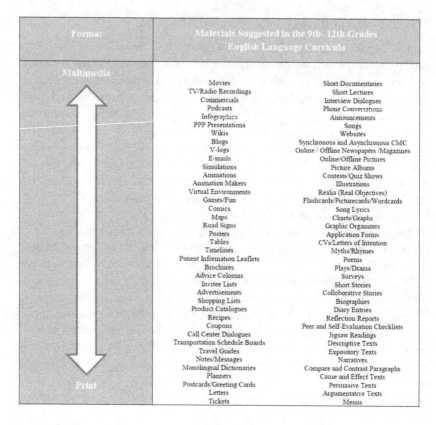

Format	Materials Suggested in the 9th–12th Grades English Language Curricula	
Multimedia ↕ Print	Movies	Short Documentaries
	TV/Radio Recordings	Short Lectures
	Commercials	Interview Dialogues
	Podcasts	Phone Conversations
	Infographics	Announcements
	PPP Presentations	Songs
	Wikis	Websites
	Blogs	Synchronous and Asynchronous CMC
	V-logs	Online / Offline Newspapers /Magazines
	E-mails	Online/Offline Pictures
	Simulations	Picture Albums
	Animations	Contests/Quiz Shows
	Animation Makers	Illustrations
	Virtual Environments	Realia (Real Objectives)
	Games/Fun	Flashcards/Picturecards/Wordcards
	Comics	Song Lyrics
	Maps	Charts/Graphs
	Road Signs	Graphic Organizers
	Posters	Application Forms
	Tables	CVs/Letters of Intention
	Timelines	Myths/Rhymes
	Patient Information Leaflets	Poems
	Brochures	Plays/Drama
	Advice Columns	Surveys
	Invitee Lists	Short Stories
	Advertisements	Collaborative Stories
	Shopping Lists	Biographies
	Product Catalogues	Diary Entries
	Recipes	Reflection Reports
	Coupons	Peer and Self-Evaluation Checklists
	Call Center Dialogues	Jigsaw Readings
	Transportation Schedule Boards	Descriptive Texts
	Travel Guides	Expository Texts
	Notes/Messages	Narratives
	Monolingual Dictionaries	Compare and Contrast Paragraphs
	Planners	Cause and Effect Texts
	Postcards/Greeting Cards	Persuasive Texts
	Letters	Argumentative Texts
	Tickets	Menus

Figure 7 Suggested Materials for 9th–12th Grades

Conclusion

In conclusion, the new English curriculum, which has been put into practice in 2018 in Turkey, is in line with CEFR standards. Starting with A1 level in the 2nd grade, it aims to reach students to B2 + when they finish high school. The curriculum has a strong emphasis on the use of ICT and developing students' communicative competence. Since communicative competence is equally critical as grammatical knowledge, the English curriculum requires teachers to utilize formative alternative assessment tools as well as traditional pen-paper exams. Increasing learners' competence in ICT is another important focus of the curriculum; hence, in formative assessment, e-portfolios and video blogs occupy a significant place. The new English curriculum has been designed with the awareness of communication across different nations and cultures. Therefore, gaining intercultural communicative competence (ICC) is also highlighted in the curriculum, which is reflected in the activities of the coursebooks by integrating cultural objects from various countries. Finally, values education also took its place in English education in Turkey by embedding the values such as justice, friendship, self-control, honesty, patience, respect, love, responsibility, patriotism, and altruism in the curriculum.

References

Biesenbach-Lucas, S. (2007). Students writing emails to faculty: An examination of e-politeness among native and non-native speakers of English. *Language Learning & Technology, 11* (2), 59–81.

Byram, M. (2000). Assessing intercultural competence in language teaching. *Sprogforum, 18,* 8–13

Cameron, L. (2001). *Teaching languages to young learners.* Cambridge: Cambridge University Press.

Chanier, T., & Selva, T. (1998). The ALEXIA System: The Use of Visual Representations to Enhance Vocabulary Learning. *Computer Assisted Language Learning, 11*(5), 489–521. Retrieved June 8, 2022 from https://www.learntech lib.org/p/88124/

Chen, C., Chen, L., & Yang, S. (2019). An English vocabulary learning app with self-regulated learning mechanism to improve learning performance and motivation. *Computer Assisted Language Learning, 32,* 237–260.

Constantinescu, A. I. (2007). Using technology to assist in vocabulary acquisition and reading comprehension. *The Internet TESL Journal,13*(2).

Council of Europe (CoE). (2001). *Common European framework of reference for languages: Learning, teaching, assessment.* Cambridge University Press.

Hale, S. L., & Cunningham, S. A. (2011). Evidence based practice using a thematic based unit for language development. Paper presented at the Texas Hearing Speech Language Association (TSHA) Annual Convention, Houston, TX.

Larsen-Freeman, D., & Anderson, M. (2011). *Techniques and principles in language teaching (3rd ed.).* Oxford University Press.

Looi, C. K., Chan, S.W., & Wu, L. (2020). Diversity and collaboration: A synthesis of differentiated development of ICT education. In: Looi C. K., Zhang H., Gao Y., & Wu L. (eds.), *ICT in education and implications for the Belt and Road Initiative.* Lecture notes in educational technology. Singapore: Springer

McKay, S. L. (2002). *Teaching English as an international language.* Oxford University Press.

Sung, Y. T., Chang, K. E., & Liu, T. C. (2016). The effects of integrating mo-
bile devices with teaching and learning on students' learning performance: A
meta-analysis and research synthesis. *Computers & Education, 94*, 252–275.

Turkey Ministry of National Education. (2018). Secondary education English
teaching program. http://mufredat.meb.gov.tr/ProgramDetay.aspx?PID=342.

Turkey Ministry of National Education. (2018). Primary education English
teaching program. http://mufredat.meb.gov.tr/ProgramDetay.aspx?PID=327.

Walker, A., & White, G. (2013). *Technology enhanced language learning: Connecting theory and practice*. Oxford University Press.

Rabia Dinçer

English Language Curriculum in Finland

English Language Education, Bahçeşehir University, Istanbul, Turkey,
rabia.dincer@bahcesehir.edu.tr

Abstract

Finland's education system has received great interest as a result of the country's performance in being one of the top achievers in the PISA scores in recent years. This international competitive success must be extensively studied in terms of its basics, which include legislation, school environment, equality, the quality of instructors, and the design of the curriculum, among others. Thus, this study set out to investigate the present foreign language education and its curriculum in basic education as an essential part of the Finnish educational organization. The educational program in Finland is explained, but the major emphasis was on compulsory education in the country, and on foreign language education at a basic level and its curriculum which are all discussed in detail.

Keywords: Finland's Education System, English Language Teaching, English Language

Introduction

Education in Finland continues to attract the attention of educators and researchers throughout the world because of its performance in being one of the top achievers in the PISA scores. Between 2000 and 2009, Finnish students achieved the highest levels of performance in reading, science, and mathematics (OECD, 2013). This worldwide competitive achievement must be thoroughly examined in terms of its fundamentals, which include policies, school conditions, equity, the quality of educators, and the design of the curriculum, among others.

Finland's success in education may be linked to a variety of dynamics. For instance, in education, long-term sustainability and consistency are two of the most crucial aspects to consider. As Sahlberg (2007) states, Finland's basic education has not undergone any significant changes since the 1970s. Instead, reforms are made at regular intervals, considering periodic needs and technological developments. The Finnish National Board of Education made the most recent revisions to the country's national curriculum in 2014 (Finnish National Agency for Education, 2018). This offers a consistent method of teaching and learning for both instructors and students. Apart from this, free education opportunities, school conditions, and teacher quality affect success in the Finnish case.

Foreign language learning is a significant issue in Finland, just as it is in other parts and topics of the educational system. Currently, English is one of the most spoken foreign languages in Finland (Statistics Finland, 2020). Most Finnish students learn English in school, and practically everyone in Finland is fluent in English, and it is used in a variety of fields in daily life, including commerce, science, culture, and the media (Jaatinen & Sarivirta, 2014). Because the nation is multilingual with its two national languages, which are Finnish and Swedish, they are more eager to acquire different languages, and as a result, they are more advantageous than monolinguals (Bialystok, 1988).

According to EU action plans and Council of Europe goals, each person must know two different languages outside their own language (Pöyhönen, 2008). Thus, Finland is an excellent example of achieving this goal. Since 71 % of the population can speak two or more languages, and 25 % can speak three or more, it is apparent that they are good at learning different languages. Finland has above-average foreign language abilities. The fact that Finland has two official languages, Finnish and Swedish, has undoubtedly affected linguistic attitudes (Statistics of Finland, 2020). Thus, Finland is one of the model nations that should be examined in terms of foreign language education, and its example should suggest some useful implications for other nations.

Finnish Education System in General

According to Sahlberg (2011), the Finnish approach to educational reform supports local and individual answers to national objectives rather than standardizing educational activities across Finland or relying on an exam-based system. This system is built on the principles of shared accountability and mutual respect (Finnish National Agency for Education, 2021a). There is a strong focus on creative learning and on strengthening all development elements, consisting of experience, knowledge and abilities, and identity and moral integrity at the same time. In Finland, there are no government standardized examinations or school inspections. The lack of these tests and inspections allows instructors greater flexibility and supports teachers to experiment with different techniques in the teaching process. Because Finland's education is widely regarded as one of the most effective globally, this strategy looks to be working exceptionally well (OECD, 2015).

The administration of national education is divided into two levels. Firstly, The Ministry of Education and Culture oversees the country's educational policies. Secondly, it is the responsibility of the Finnish National Agency for Education to ensure that the policy objectives are met. It collaborates with the Ministry of Education to design educational goals, content, and techniques for early childhood, pre-primary, elementary, secondary, and adult education programs (Finnish National Agency for Education, 2014). Municipalities, the most popular types of local authorities, are in charge of administering the local areas. They make choices on the distribution of funds, the development of local curricula, and the hiring of personnel. The towns also have the authority to assign decision-making authority to the schools if they so choose. Thus, the staff in some schools can decide and design their own curriculum regarding the national curriculum's standards.

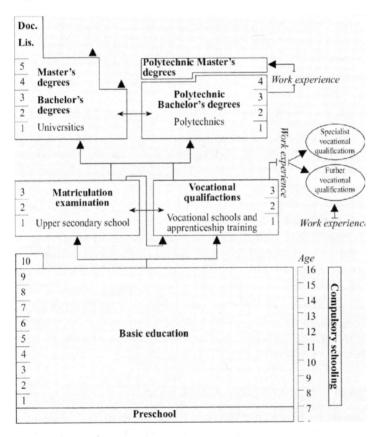

Figure 1 The framework of the Finnish Educational System

As seen in Figure 1, the Finnish educational system consists of the following components: early childhood education, pre-primary education, basic education, general upper secondary education, vocational education, and higher education. All children between the ages of 6 and 15 are required to attend compulsory schooling. Pre-primary, elementary, and upper secondary education are all included. Following 9 years of basic education, students may pursue general upper secondary education or vocational education. Upper secondary school leads to the matriculation test, whereas vocational education leads to a vocational certification. A single structure system known as basic education is used to deliver compulsory schooling to all students. It consists of students in grades 1 through 9. Pre-primary and elementary education are provided at no cost to students. Pupils also get free study materials, a daily school lunch, health and social services, as well as transportation from home to school if the walk to school is too far or too unsafe (National Core Curriculum for Basic Education – NCCBE, 2014). In this report, the focus will be on basic education curricula, specifically foreign language education in the basic education curriculum.

Language Teaching System in Finland for Basic Education

Foreign language education is a requirement at every step of the system. One of the languages must be the national languages of the country, which are Swedish or Finnish. Besides this, one additional foreign language must be studied. Language studies begin at the earliest in the 3rd grade when a child is 9 years old. At each level, students may choose to study a foreign language as an elective.

Overall, the Finnish educational system ensures that its students have a linguistic repertoire that consists of a minimum of three languages: their mother tongue; the second national language; and one additional foreign language, which is often English. These three languages are spoken by over 80 % of Finns. As evidenced by statistics, language learning is becoming increasingly centered on the three languages listed above, and it is generally believed to be no longer as advantageous as it once was, if not outright unnecessary. Learning another language other than English, on the other hand, may be a necessity (Finnish National Agency for Education, 2021a).

Finland's Foreign Language Curriculum

The National Core Curriculum for Basic Education serves as the foundation for Finnish primary school language education. Finns follow a core curriculum developed by NCCBE, the most recent edition of which was published in 2014. Some of the primary objectives of the latest reform include boosting child engagement, improving the authenticity of learning, and enabling each kid to be successful in their education (NCCBE, 2014). The students put objectives, solve problems, and evaluate their own learning in relation to the goals they have set. In addition, in all courses, there is a greater emphasis on ICT skills, plurilingualism, multiculturalism, well-being, and everyday life management (Finnish National Agency for Education, 2021a). As can be seen in Figure 2, the new core curriculum focuses a strong emphasis on the development of transversal competencies in the classroom. A changing society necessitates the development of ever- increasing transversal skills and competencies. As a result, it is critical that each topic encourages the development of cross-disciplinary competencies.

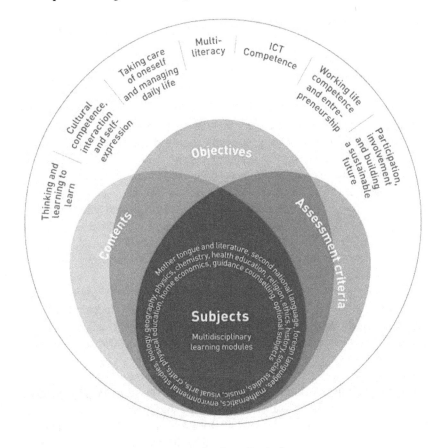

Figure 2 Transversal Competencies in the Core Curriculum

Finnish National Core Curriculum is divided into three major categories. First and foremost, it is an administrative file, and it is a component of the national system for organizing and managing education. Second, it is an intellectual record that defines and recreates contextually meaningful information, and in this way, it shows contemporary concepts of knowledge. In a third sense, it is a pedagogical text, offering guidance and assistance to instructors while also establishing standards for education (Vitikka et al., 2012). Local sustainers of education have a great deal of flexibility in developing their municipal and school curricula on their own terms, as long as they do it in compliance with the nationally standardized core curriculum. The local curriculum must consider the requirements and facilities of the community, as well as the local environment (Niemi, 2012). The core curriculum does not address issues such as instructional techniques and educational practices.

Apart from this national curriculum, institutions and municipalities are required to develop their curriculum as part of their responsibility. The localized curriculum is also highly broad in design, allowing for considerable flexibility in how they are implemented. Teachers, therefore, have a great deal of discretion in determining their own techniques, approaches, and instructional resources.

To provide a brief overview of language instruction in Finnish basic education, there are four distinct syllabi, two of which are mandatory and the other two are optional. The mandatory syllabi are as follows: When it comes to the A1 syllabus, it is required and normally starts in the 3rd grade with 2 hours a week. The medium of instruction is usually English (Finnish for Swedish-speaking Finns). French, German, or Russian are generally included in the A2 curriculum, which is an optional language that begins most commonly in grades 3–6 and is usually referred to as A2 (English for Swedish-speaking Finns). The B1 syllabus is the second obligatory language syllabus, and it starts in the 6th grade and continues through the 12th grade. Unless the learner has already studied the second national language as part of an A1 or A2 curriculum, it is normally the second national language, such as Swedish or Finnish. B2 is an optional foreign language that may be taken starting in 7th grade. When it comes to foreign language introduction and instruction in Finnish basic education, there is some variation amongst schools in terms of how, when, and to what degree foreign languages are taught. In Finland, the most common foreign language that is taught is English. According to Statistics Finland(2020), the number of students learning English in grades 1–6 grew in 2020 as compared to the previous year. A total of 93 % of students in grades 1 through 6 took English as a subject. Compared to the previous year, the proportion of students in grades 1–6 who studied English climbed by 10 % points. Almost all pupils in grades 7–9 took English as a subject.

Generally, foreign language studies in Finnish schools begin in the 3rd grade; however, depending on the school setting, education may begin earlier in the 1st or 2nd grade. In that case, language instruction aligns with the core curriculum. Thus, the main aim of language education at that stage is to give a preliminary introduction to meet different languages (English mostly). According to the core curriculum (NCCBE, 2014), listening, comprehension, and vocabulary skills are emphasized in grades 1–2. It is also expected that this would inspire students to use the target language in a practical and imaginative manner via games and rhymes, among other things. The focus is not only on language use but also on the improvement of basic language study abilities and the development of genuine enthusiasm in language acquisition. The content topics are relevant to the interests of the students as well as their daily lives, such as at home and school. Language learning should also promote developing a plurilingual and multicultural identity.

The main purposes of teaching for grades 3–6 are separated into three main content areas: the first two of them are related to raising awareness towards cultural diversity and language learning skills, and the third area is mainly about linguistic competencies which are categorized as developing language proficiency in terms of interaction skills, text interpretation, and production skills. The sample objectives in each of these content areas are presented in Figure 3. Daily living, the surrounding environment, and a broad understanding of the target language culture are all covered in a manner that is comparable to that taught in the 1st and 2nd grades.

New topics include, for example, how to conduct business in a variety of scenarios and how to understand one's own cultural background. In addition, the present edition of the core curriculum emphasizes the integration of information and communication technology (ICT), which assists students in developing their skills for integration and active engagement in a global community (Finnish National Agency for Education, 2021).

Objectives of instruction	Content areas related to the objectives	Transversal competences
Growing into cultural diversity and language awareness		
O1 to guide the pupil to notice the linguistic and cultural richness of his or her surroundings and the world, and the status of English as a language of global communication	C1	T2
Language-learning skills		
O5 to explore the objectives of the instruction jointly and to create a permissive classroom atmosphere in	C2	T1, T3
Evolving language proficiency, text interpretation skills		
O10 to guide the pupil to work with spoken and written texts with many different levels of difficulty, using different comprehension strategies	C3	T4
Evolving language proficiency, text production skills		
O11 to offer the pupil opportunities for producing speech and writing on a wider range of topics, also paying attention to essential structures and the basic rules of pronunciation	C3	T3, T4, T5, T7

Figure 3 Samples of Objectives in English in Grades 3–6

Furthermore, regarding studying methods to achieve these objectives, some significant dynamics are emphasized in the core curriculum. For instance, pair or group works, collaboration with instructors, and various techniques such as gamification and drama are suggested in the core curriculum. Additionally, pupils are guided to use different channels and instructional technologies to meet objectives.

The evaluation, on the other hand, is motivating and gives an opportunity for students to become aware of and enhance their talents. The European Language Portfolio, for instance, may be used as an evaluation instrument for grades 3–6.

As a means of achieving the above-mentioned objectives and of evaluating language studies, the curriculum includes an assessment scale of what constitutes satisfactory performance by the time students reach the end of primary school (grade 6). As the foundation for the Finnish application, well-developed performance is characterized specifically for each part of linguistic competencies (see Table 1), such as communication skills, written or spoken text comprehension, and production, using the proficiency scale of the Common European Framework of Reference for Languages (CEFR). The goal of elementary-level foreign language instruction is to achieve the levels of a basic user, in the target language. Basic levels are further subdivided into more specific levels in the Finnish application. The same is true for levels A2.1 and A2.2. Chapter 14 of the National Core Curriculum contains detailed definitions of these concepts (NCCBE, 2014).

Table 1 Good Performance of Linguistic Competency in English as Targeted at Grade 6

Interaction Skills	Text Interpretation Skills	Text Production Skills
A2.1	A2.1	A2.1
The initial phase of basic language proficiency	The initial phase of basic language proficiency	The initial phase of basic language proficiency

As can be seen in Table 1, "good performance" in the target language at the end of grade 6 targets level A2.1 for all aspects of language proficiency. The pupils practice listening, speaking, reading, and writing on various topics including their family, friends and social environments, and hobbies (NCCBE, 2014).

The objectives of the instruction for 7–9 grades are to guide the students in pursuing the language level gained in grades 3–6 and improving their high-order thinking skills while learning the target language. The content is chosen from the perspective of the students, taking into consideration their interest areas, orientation to secondary school, the linguistic skills required in their career, and studies of the students' involvement and agency on a local and global scale (NCCBE, 2014). The goal of the instruction in grades 7–9 in language instruction is to achieve the levels of fluent user, B1.1, in the target language.

Objective of instruction	Content areas	Assessment targets in the subject	Knowledge and skills for the grade 8
O7 to support the pupil's initiative in communicating, using compensation, and negotiating meaning	C3	Using communication strategies	The pupil is somewhat able to take initiative in the different stages of communication, knows how to verify whether the communication partner has understood the message, and has learned to compensate or replace an unknown word or rephrase his or her message. The pupil is able to negotiate the meanings of unknown expressions.
O8 to help the pupil recognise cultural features in communication and to support the pupil in constructive intercultural communication	C3	Cultural appropriateness of communication	The pupil indicates that he or she knows the most important rules of politeness. The pupil is able to take into account some key perspectives related to cultural practices in his or her interaction.
Evolving language proficiency, text interpretation skills			**Level of proficiency B1.1**
O9 to offer the pupil opportunities for reading and listening to versatile standard-language and popularised texts from various sources and to interpret them using different strategies	C3	Text interpretation skills	The pupil understands the main ideas and some details of clear, nearly regular-tempo, standard language speech and popularised written text. The pupil understands speech or written text based on a shared experience or general knowledge. The pupil is able to find the main ideas, keywords, and important details without preparation.

Figure 4 Objectives of Instruction in the Syllabus in English in Grades 7–9

Overall, the aim and objectives of foreign language education in the curriculum are shaped according to the ages and needs of the students. Every topic makes use of linguistic and cultural knowledge, for example, interdisciplinary learning modules in basic education and theme studies in upper secondary school. Linguistic and cultural knowledge are used in every subject. Students learn how to utilize languages as a tool for supporting their learning in a variety of topic areas. The notion of active agency is a major concept in the most recent national core curriculum, and it refers to the readiness and desire to engage, influence, and act in a democratic society (NCCBE, 2014). It is possible to increase active agency in the learning process by bringing an interactive, exploratory working technique to learning, and by presenting students with a (linguistically) exciting learning environment to enhance authenticity (İrican, 2017).

To sum up, when the foreign language curriculum is examined holistically, it is apparent that its objectives and content areas are relevant to the general aims of the core curriculum. For instance, transversal skills and competencies are also implemented in foreign language curricula for all grades at different levels as well as linguistic competencies (NCCBE, 2014). The transversal skills like ICT use, multiculturalism, multilingualism, learning to learn, and self-autonomy are included and pointed at each level in the language curriculum. Thus, the local curriculum, classroom activities, syllabuses, instructional designs, teaching techniques, and methods are developed regarding these main objectives.

Conclusion

Finland is attempting to do something that no other nation has ever done before. It is Finland's goal to develop students who are computer literate, have intercultural competencies, are multiliterate, are self-sufficient in both their personal lives and their academic lives, respect other people's ideas, are tolerant of other people's beliefs, and are aware of what is going on in the world (İrican, 2017). Basic education English courses are intended to educate students not just on the fundamentals of English communication but also to expose them to a variety of multidisciplinary topics and situations that are widely recognized as major issues across the globe.

References

Bialystock, E. (1988). Levels of bilingualism and levels of linguistic awareness. *Development Psychology, 24*(4), 560–567.

Finnish National Agency for Education (EDUFI). (2014). *National core curriculum for preprimary education.*Publications 2016:6. Helsinki.Finnish National Agency for Education.

Finnish National Agency for Education (EDUFI). (2018). *National core curriculum in early childhood education and care.* Regulations and guidelines 2018:3c. Helsinki.Finnish National Agency for Education.

Finnish National Agency for Education.(2021a).*National Core Curriculum for Basic Education.* Retrieved December 10, 2021, from https:// www.oph.fi/en/ education-and-qualifications/national-core-curriculum-basic-education.

Finnish National Agency for Education.(2021b). *New national core curriculum for basic education: focus on school culture and integrative approach.* Retrieved December 10, 2021, from https://www.oph.%/en/statistics-and-publications/ publications/new-national-core-curriculum-basic-education-focus-school

İrican, E. S. (2017). A comparative study on basic education curricula of Finland and Turkey in foreign language teaching. *International Journal of Curriculum and Instruction, 9*(2), 137–156.

Jaatinen, R., & Saarivirta, T. (2014). The evolution of English Language teaching during societal transition in Finland – A mutual relationship or a distinctive process? *Australian Journal of Teacher Education, 39*(11), 29–44.

National Core Curriculum for Basic Education – NCCBE (2021). Finnish National Agency for Education. Retrieved December 10, 2021, from https://www.oph.fi/en/education-and-qualifications/national-core-curriculum-basic-education.

Niemi, R. (2012). *The teacher as an implementer of curriculum change. A casestudy analysis of small rural schools in Finland. Transforming teachers' work globally: In search of a better way for schools and their communities.* Rotterdam: Sense Publishers, pp. 111–147.

OECD. (2013). *Education policy outlook: Finland.* Paris: OECD Publishing.

OECD. (2015). *Education policy outlook: Finland.* Paris: OECD Publishing.

Pöyhönen, S. (2008). Foreign language teaching in basic and secondary education in Finland: Current situation and future challenges. Invited keynote paper presented at congress: Apprendimento delle lingue straniere e la formazion e degli insegnanti, Rovereto, IPRASE del Trentino, Italy, 15.3.2008.

Sahlberg, P. (2007). Education policies for raising student learning: The Finnish approach. *Journal of Education Policy, 22*(2), 147–171.

Sahlberg, P. (2011). The fourth way of Finland. *Journal of educational change, 12*(2), 173–185.

Statistics Finland – Subject choices of students 2020. (2021, October 14). Statistics Finland. https://www.stat.fi/til/ava/2020/01/ava_2020_01_2021-10-14_tie_001_en.html

Vitikka, E., Krokfors, L., & Hurmerinta, E. (2012). The Finnish national core curriculum. In *Miracle of education.* Sense Publishers, pp. 83–96.

Kevser Kaya

English Language Curriculum in France

English Language Education, Bahçeşehir University, Istanbul, Turkey,
kevser.kaya1@bahcesehir.edu.tr

Abstract

France is known for having advocated for language ecology in its language-in-education regulations and public rhetoric. It offers a large array of foreign languages. The purpose of this chapter is to examine whether the vast spectrum of choices and state propaganda in favor of linguistic diversity corresponds with a considerable variety of languages being taught. The position of English among these languages, as well as the actual implementation of English language teaching, is particularly explored. To create a general understanding, the chapter first presents the French school system and curriculum. The place of foreign languages especially English in French curriculum and English language curriculum in specific the first 3 years of Cycle 2 (primary school) are stated.

Keywords: English curriculum, French education system, primary school, interculturality

Introduction

The French educational system was based on broad concepts inspired by the Revolution of 1789, and it has been supplemented and influenced by a collection of legal writings ranging from the 19th century to the present day (Eurydice, 2021). The French education system is recognized by a strong central state presence in education organization and funding. The Department of National Education, Higher Education, and Research monitors the French educational system. It governs within the framework established by Parliament, which establishes the fundamental principles of education. Because the French education system is centralized, the state plays a significant role in governance. The details of curricula at all levels of education are designed; the teachers' admissions procedure is organized, content is designed, and instructors who become civil servants are recruited and offered in-service training; inspectors who are responsible for monitoring the quality of the education system are recruited and trained by the state (Eurydice, 2021). Even though most French schools adhere to a national curriculum created by the Ministry of Education, the government began letting schools determine 20 % of the curriculum as part of changes in May 2015. The changes also put a lot of emphasis on studying languages (Bird, Simmons & Ellenburg, 2019).

The vision of the French educational system is that education is a global common good. Access to quality education for all, respectful of cultural and linguistic diversity, is a factor of individual emancipation, improvement of collective living conditions, social inclusion, and economic development (MEN, 2021). Skills are defined by a shared core of knowledge, skills, and culture, which is based on information in various disciplines that a student must master by the completion of obligatory schooling. During the second and third cycles of basic education (the elementary school), children develop a shared culture.

Organization of the French School System

The French school system, like that of most European countries, can be roughly separated into two sections: primary and secondary. The national curriculum is further split into five cycles across schools within this established division (which are frequently geographically separated).

- Cycle2 begins with the preparatory course and ends with CE2.
- Cycle 3, which includes the last two grades of elementary school (CM1 and CM2) and the grade secondary school's 1st grade (6th).
- Cycle 4, which spans the final three grades of mandatory schooling (5th, 4th, and 3rd).
- A cycle terminal that spans 3 years of upper secondary school (high school) (MEN, 2021).

The Primary School

The primary goal of the first 3 years of kindergarten is to familiarize students with the school setting. The instructional technique allows children to grow as individuals and learn to work as part of a team. To achieve this, they learn through play, problem-solving, creativity, and memory exercises. Teaching is usually divided into five categories as expression and language, physical exercises, artistic pursuits, organizing thoughts, and exploring the world.

Primary school students receive instruction for a total of 24 hours per week. The school year consists of 864 hours of mandatory education. If each domain's global instruction time is honored, the weekly teaching schedule can be changed as needed for educational projects led by the teaching staff. Furthermore, in elementary education, 15-minute breaks must be included in the timetable in a balanced manner across all instructional domains (Eurydice, 2021).

In the international context of teaching current foreign languages, specific courses are offered. These are electives and offered to any willing student in schools that provide them beginning in CE1. These lessons last 1h 30 every week, in addition to the 24 hours of mandatory schooling. These lessons are taught by foreign teachers who are fluent in French and are provided by partner countries.

Teachers in elementary schools must adhere to a national educational program. Children begin acquiring a second language in their early years (CP, CE1, CE2). They are also encouraged to ask questions and participate in activities such as art, music, and sports. Moral and civic education are also introduced to them. History, geography, physics, and art history are taught later in CM1 and CM2 (Dimitrijevic, 2021).

The primary school runs from 3 to 11 years old and is divided into two parts: the kindergarten from 3 to 6, and the elementary school from 6 to 11, that is, the start of mandatory education, though most children go to school kindergarten first. The elementary school is further divided into two cycles:

- 2nd cycle, which runs from the kindergarten's final class through the first 3 years of elementary school (Preparatory course, or CP, and elementary course 1 and 2, or CE1 and 2). This cycle emphasizes "fundamental learning," which consists of a foreign language (generally but not mandatorily English).
- 3rd cycle, which includes the final two grades of elementary school (average course, CM1 and 2) as well as the first grade of college (6th). A compulsory foreign language is required once again, which is generally, but not always, English. Pupils are to achieve A1 by the end of 6th year (Cambridge, 2016).

The Secondary School

The college lasts 4 years from the ages of 11–15 (classes 6th, 5th, 4th, and 3rd).

Students take the national diploma of the patent at the end of college, which includes two foreign languages, one of which is almost always English. At the patent, students are expected to achieve A2. The high school, which lasts 3 years (the second, first, and the last), culminates in the general high school with the bachelor's that includes examinations in two foreign languages, one of which is almost always English. Students need to achieve CEFR level B2. Students decide their specialization in the first year and may then attend a general high school, a technological high school, or a vocational high school. All include a foreign language. Second grade marks the end of the common base, the curricula that include mandatory secondary education till the age of 16. The common base's English exit level is B1. At the end of the second year, students select their specialties (science, social science, or literature). The last two grades of high school are the last cycle, and the curricula direct to the bachelor's test. A speaking test in a foreign language, generally English, with a target score of C1 has been included in the literary option since 2013 (Cambridge, 2016).

Assessment in General

Grade 1 (Preparatory course), Grade 2 (Elementary course), Grade 4 (1), Grade 6 (sixth), and Grade 10 (Sixth) have statutory assessments at the beginning of the academic year (Second). Students take four written examinations in French, Mathematics, History, and Sciences, as well as a presenting project and an interview at the end of Grade 9 (Third). Students must complete the legal criteria, but their academic performance does not influence their future educational possibilities. The national diploma is awarded to successful students. Students take the general bachelor's degree, a national standardized evaluation required for further education, at the completion of Grade 12 (the final year). Students are given a single bachelor diploma upon graduation, which lists all the subjects they studied and their grades in each. Although there are no standardized tests, there is constant and periodic assessment.

A special report is given to the parents about their kid's progress three times a year (schoolbook). The marking method is commonly indicated by a notation such as "not achieved," "partially achieved," "achieved," or "excelled." The school holds meetings on a regular basis (generally two or three times a year) and meetings (if required either from the instructor or their parents). Pupils take an exam to acquire the national diploma at the end of the third year, which evaluates their knowledge and abilities acquired in lower secondary school. It contains written exams in French, math, civic education, history, and geography and an oral test in art history that evaluates these courses. Students take the bachelor test, which is the first higher education diploma, at the completion of the last grade of secondary school the last year. The bachelor's degree permits the recipient to enroll in the first year of university study.

There are three primary alternatives:

Scientific series: The natural sciences, physics, and mathematics are studied.
Economic and social series: Economics, history, geography, social sciences, and mathematics are studied.
Literary series: French, foreign languages, philosophy, foreign literature, and the arts are studied (MEN, 2021).

The Place of English in the French School System

To be able to have an understanding of English in the French school system, it is of value to mention how English started to be studied as a foreign language. The modern foreign language teaching in elementary education in France underwent a controlled experimental project beginning in 1989, but it was optional and only involved a small number of schools. The French Ministry of Education's centralism, Jacobinism, the idea of national monolingualism, and even linguistic protectionism have all historically been strong opponents of language acquisition, just like they have been in the United Kingdom (Duverger, 2009). This situation, however, was ended by Jack Lang, France's then-socialist Minister of Education. "In the future, our goal is for each child to learn two modern languages, at an age when the quality of his/her musical ear is at its peak, In Year 6, students will begin learning a second foreign language," said Jack Lang in a public speech on foreign language teaching in primary education delivered in January 2001 (Lang, 2001, as cited in Salomon, 2018). Lang then instituted a slew of new measures aimed at improving the teaching of a foreign language in primary school. Foreign languages were now considered a legitimate course in primary school, with the curriculum spanning primary school and the first year of middle school. Although Lang believed that children should be exposed to English at some point in their education, he supported other European languages and local French languages as well, so fostering the nation's linguistic variety. Among them were the languages of Breton (Celtic), Basque (Vasconic), Occitan (Romance), and Alsatian (Germanic). Only 24 % of elementary school kids were studying a language other than English in 2001, which he bemoaned. A much more concerning statistic was that only 10 % of students in Year 1 of lower secondary school were studying a different foreign language than English (Lang, 2001, as cited in Salomon, 2018). That was a major reform to strengthen the teaching of foreign languages from preschool to university. For the very first time, it was claimed that France was no longer a monolingual country, and regional languages were recognized as depicting a personal and collective wealth that should be appreciated by the education system. Under the impacts of some of the Council of Europe's work, such as the Common European Framework for Languages, the European Year of Languages, and the European Portfolio, concepts such as Europe's cultural and linguistic diversity and the endorsement of plurilingualism became part of the French state's linguistic policies (Helot & Young, 2005).

France urgently needed to enhance its English skills, according to a report from the private language instruction company Education First published in

November 2014. The research continued by stating that France had compara-
tively poor English language proficiency compared to other European nations,
suggesting that France was more focused on preserving its own language and
culture than acquiring English. But when it comes to selecting their first different language to study at school, most of the students prefer English. English
is prominently featured in the curricula across obligatory schooling, colleges,
and universities both state-run and private adult education. There are over
500 private language schools in Paris alone that teach English to both children
and adults (Bird, Simmons & Ellenburg, 2019). Though English is not a compulsory language, it is the most preferred language of all. Students can select
from 56 languages: Albanian, German, Amharic, English, Arabic, Armenian,
Bambara, Basque, Berber, Breton, Bulgarian, Cambodian, Catalan, Chinese,
Korean, Corsican, Creole, Croatian, Danish, Spanish, Estonian, Finnish, Gallo,
Modern Greek, Hausa, Hebrew, Hindi, Hungarian, Indonesian-Malay, Italian,
Japanese, Melanesian languages, regional languages of Alsace and Moselle, La-
otian, Lithuanian, Macedonian, Malagasy, Dutch, Norwegian, Occitan-Langue
d'Oc, Persian, Peul, Polish, Portuguese, Romanian, Russian, Serbian, Slovak,
Slovenian, Swedish, Swahili, Tahitian, Tamil, Czech, Turkish, and Vietnamese
(Fullbright,2011). Starting with the CP class in primary school, students must
learn a modern language.

In the international framework of teaching modern foreign languages, specific courses are offered. These are optional and open to any willing student in
schools that offer such courses beginning in CE1. These classes total 1h30 per
week, in addition to the 24 hours of compulsory schooling. Such classes are
taught by foreign teachers who speak fluent French and are supplied by partner
countries (Eurydice, 2021).

The English Language Curriculum

There is a national foreign language curriculum that each school and instructor
adapt to fit their individual teaching methods and pupils. It then includes two
parts: content, which is very broadly specified, and Common European Framework of Reference (CEFR) levels as targets for each stage (MEN, 2021). For instance, the material for pupils in the 16–18 age range is divided into four main
categories: spaces and exchanges, notions of progress, myths and heroes, and
places and forms of power. This variety allows teachers a lot of freedom to choose
subjects that pupils will find interesting or valuable. The five components of the
program are reading, presentations, interactive speaking, listening comprehension, and written comprehension. The methods used to teach languages shift as

the politicians in charge do, but project-based learning, sometimes known as the "actionnelle action approach," has recently taken the lead. A vigorous campaign to abandon "chalk and talk" has been supported by the government and academies. This is creating a schism between new teaching grads who wish to use what they have acquired and academic administrative people who have long practiced "teaching from a textbook" (Bird, Simmons & Ellenburg, 2019).

English Teaching in the Elementary Schools in France

Cycle 2 is the starting point for learning modern languages for all students with a teaching corresponding to the A1 level at the oral level of the Framework Common European Reference for Languages (CEFR). This cycle contributes to laying the foundations for the first development of multilingual competence of raise. Oral language is the priority.

Cycle 3 is the continuation of pupils' learning of a foreign or regional language which they begin in cycle 2. In cycle 3 the aim is to achieve a uniform level of competence in all language activities and to develop a greater mastery of some of them. This is for all students to reach at least the A1 level of the CEFR in the five language activities. Activity is not limited to level A1 because level A2 can be achieved by many students in several language activities. In short, the overall goal is for all students to achieve at least A1 in all five language skills by the end of 6th grade with some also expected to achieve A2.

The English Language Syllabus in Cycle 2

The following syllabus presents a general framework of the English language in Cycle 2 regarding listening, speaking, taking part in interactions, and reading-writing skills (Cambridge, 2016).

Listening

- Understanding oral English.

Expected at the end of the cycle: Understand familiar words and very common expressions about yourself, your family, and the concrete and immediate environment if people speak slowly and distinctly. Follow short and simple instructions. The elementary repertoire of words and expressions regarding simple concrete situations.

Knowledge and skills associated: Examples of situations, activities, and resources for the student. Understand the instructions for the class. Use a few familiar words and some very common expressions run. Follow the thread of a very short story. Examples of situations, activities, and resources. Language exposure activities in various culturally identifiable contexts, corresponding to the concerns of students of this age, in using digital tools, listening to the playback of albums, nursery rhymes, or songs, in viewing short excerpts of animated drawings. Individual apprehension of the sound document and pooling to identify and restore its meaning explicitly, without prohibiting the use of language French if necessary. Identification of some simple contrasts in the functioning of the oral language.

Progressivity benchmarks: At the CP the students discover and learn to use the classroom instructions, some familiar words, and some very common expressions (formulas of encouragement and congratulation, name, age, politeness formulas, etc.). They can follow the thread of a very short story adapted to their age, with appropriate aids and very simple instructions (clapping hands and getting up). At CE1, they consolidate this knowledge by enriching the lexicon: they can include a dozen instructions, use expressions familiar and everyday as well as very simple statements that aim to situate and describe their close environment (place of residence, e.g.). They can follow three or four instructions relating to gestures and body movement and listen to the playback of an album suitable for their age. At CE2, students introduce themselves or someone and reply when someone asks simple questions about themselves, for example, about their place of residence.

Speaking

• Talking continuously (long turn)

Expected at the end of the cycle: Use simple expressions and phrases to describe yourself, the place, and people from the surrounding area.

Knowledge and skills associated: Reproduce an oral model. Use short expressions or phrases close to the models encountered during apprenticeships to describe oneself. Read aloud a brief text expressively. Telling a short story from images or models already met. An elementary repertoire of words on the places of habitation and people from the entourage of the child. The syntax of the description is simple (places, spaces, person).

Examples of situations, activities, and resources for the student: Activities to report on the diversity of the languages spoken. Activities that allow the use of the language in situations analogous to situations already meet. Students analyze and evaluate their own language practice and that of their comrades live or from recordings sound. Songs or nursery rhymes and sketches made from excerpts from albums or youth films, and games.

Progressivity benchmarks: At the CP, students must reproduce a simple oral model taken from a nursery rhyme, a song, or a story and use one or two expressions or phrases close to the models encountered during learning to describe themselves (name, age). At CE1, students can reproduce a short excerpt from a nursery rhyme, a song, a poem, or a history. They present themselves independently by saying their name, surname, age, and place residential. At CE2, they reproduce the date, short nursery rhymes, songs, and poems. After training, they read aloud short texts and tell a short story and stereotyped by using a few images.

- Taking part in interactions

Expected at the end of the cycle: Ask simple questions on familiar topics or on what we need immediately need, as well as answer such questions.

Knowledge and skills associated: Welcome. Introduce yourself. Ask someone about his news and to react, to hear from him. Formulate basic wishes. Use polite formulas. Answering questions on topics familiar. Spell familiar words and names. An elementary repertoire of words on familiar topics. The syntax of the conversation is simple question type/response. Communication situations.

Examples of situations, activities, and student resources: Role-playing games. Recording and re-listening what is said in order to analyze and evaluate his own practice of the language. Electronic exchanges within the framework of projects, a work around a youth album, of nursery rhymes, songs, and poems.

Progressivity benchmarks: At the CP, students learn to repeat basic dialogues of class rituals. In doing so, they begin to engage in dialogue by asking for news and reacting. They begin to use formulas of politeness. It is at CE2 that students can engage in a very short conversation that allows them to reinvest the lexicon related to the presentation of oneself and someone, use simple formulas of politeness, apologize, spell simple and transparent words, and respond to a few questions to communicate in a simple way if the interlocutor speaks slowly and distinctly and is cooperative.

Since the curricula aim to increase communicative skills, more impromptu opportunities for discussion and interaction would help in learning and maybe boost learning.

Reading and Writing

There is no syllabus for writing or reading comprehension in Cycle 2. This illustrates how valuable spoken language is.

It seems improbable that teachers are not giving learners opportunities to read and write at the most basic level in action, although reading and writing are not prioritized at this grade in the French curricula.

Conclusion

France has a long history of being a powerful nation with a strong national identity that has spread its own language and cultural values throughout the world. However, English has emerged as a major competitor to French's global dominance. The most outstanding result of this report is the large array of languages presented to students as a foreign language. This may stem from the tremendous social push to improve foreign language instruction, as well as diversification to counteract the hegemony of English. The inclusion of regional languages, as well as some commonly spoken non-European languages such as Arabic, Chinese, and Russian, may have been proposed to diversify the languages given in the primary curriculum. On the surface, it appears that children entering primary school have a wide range of languages to choose from, and therefore France is perceived as engaging in European efforts to safeguard minority languages, which are essentially regional languages. Diversification seems to have remained in a few phrases sprinkled throughout the curriculum emphasizing the importance of linguistic and cultural variety.

Regarding the interculturality that was a major focus of the curriculum, it is significant to note that MEN values diversity in the teaching of early foreign languages education. Learning a foreign or a regional language also promotes children to learn about the benefits of being exposed to many cultures, languages, and people in general. It doesn't seem to suggest a different ideological stance within primary language education. This emphasis on the languages spoken by students is a step towards recognizing home languages and, thus, multilingualism. It might be a strategy to create a multilingual learning environment in the normally monolingual French classroom while simultaneously laying the foundation for intercultural education.

References

Bird, S., Simmons, R., & Ellenburg, G. (2019). Learning English (and French) in France. *Language Issues: The ESOL Journal, 30*(2), 53–56.

Cambridge. (2016). Comparison of the language tested in Cambridge English examinations with the content of the national English-teaching curriculum in French schools. https://www.cambridgeenglish.org

Dimitrijevic, U. (2021). *The French Education System*. Expatica. https://www.expatica.com/fr/education/chilren-education/french-education-system-101147

Duverger, J. (2009). École élémentaire et enseignement des langues. *Tréma*, (28), 17–22. https://doi.org/10.4000/trema.259

Eurydice (2021). Key Features of the Education System, France. https:/a.eu/natio nal-policies/eurydice/france-en

Fullbright (2011). Fullbright France Commission Franco-Americaine. https://fulbright-france.org/docs/2011154845_GUIDECOMMONAPP2011.pdf

Hélot, C., & Young, A. (2005). The notion of diversity in language education: Policy and practice at primary level in France. *Language, culture and curriculum, 18*(3), 242–257. https://doi.org/10.1080/07908310508668745

MEN. (2021). Ministère de l'Education nationale et du Ministère de l'Enseignement supérieure et de la Recherche. Bulletin Officiel spécial – Programmes d'enseignement du cycle des apprentissages fondamentaux (cycle 2), du cycle de consolidation (cycle 3) et du cycle des approfondissements (cycle 4). https://www.education.gouv.fr

Salomon, J. K. P. (2018). Current trends in teaching English as a foreign language. The case of French primary schools. *Edu lingua (4)*1. DOI:10.14232/edulingua.2018.1.3

Nurhan Çökmez

English Language Curriculum in Germany

English Language Education, Bahçeşehir University, Istanbul, Turkey, nurhan.cokmez@bahcesehir.edu.tr

Abstract

Germany, with the highest population rate in Europe, has been criticized sharply for its education system, especially after disappointing international test results, which have resulted in several reforms. The most recent reform has been introduced by the standing conference KMK in the year 2016, and all the states had to revise their curricula according to the newly adopted strategy of digitalization. The states and schools have been able to adjust their program according to their needs as the curriculum provides an overall framework with general objectives. This decentralized and multi-track school system of Germany makes it quite complex to evaluate in a unit form. However, this chapter aims to examine especially the English language program implemented at the primary school level in the state of Saxony. The approaches adopted and innovations addressed are included as it sheds light on a decentralized system with high achievement of English language proficiency among students.

Keywords: Germany, primary school, EFL, curriculum

Introduction

Germany is a federal republic with a population of 83.129.285 citizens. The federal statistical office reports that 11.4 million of the total population consists of foreigners and 21.9 million of the citizens have a migration background (Destatis, 2021a). The statistical data demonstrates that Germany is a thickly populated country with a considerable number of citizens with a migration background. Due to the ever-growing migration rate especially in European Union countries, the case of Germany presents implications for several issues including education. The average age of people with a migration background is 35.6, whereas citizens' age without a migration background is 47.3 in average. The lower age rate of migrants clearly has an impact on sociodemographic features (Destatis, 2021b).

Due to the administrative structure of the country, Germany delegates the responsibility of educational and cultural planning to the 16 states and their parliaments. Thus, the states which are called *Länder* have autonomy regarding their education systems (Phillips, 1995). However, the coordination of policies among the states is prosecuted by federal planning and policy bodies called *Kulturministerkonferenz*, acronym KMK (the standing conference for ministers of education). This body regulates the main educational policy; therefore, states cannot drift apart from the education system exerting limitless authority.

The Education System in Germany

Compulsory education starts with the age of 6 years and continues for 9 years (in some states it is 10 years). The first 4 years of education are performed at primary school which are named *Grundschule*. In the states of Berlin and Brandenburg, primary education extends through grade 6. After primary education students are distributed among the various types of secondary schools in accordance with recommendations offered by primary school teachers. Thus, the secondary education system, which starts at grade 5, or grade 7 in the aforementioned states, is rather complex. The main school types are *Hauptschule*, *Realschule* and *Gymnasium* (Auernheimer, 2005). After the compulsory full-time training period, students who do not prefer to pursue a full-time general or vocational education have to attend school part-time to receive vocational training. The duration of the training is variable and depends on the type of apprenticeship (Pluntke, 2013).

Germany is the most populous nation in the European Union and possesses one of the largest economies (Eurostat, 2021). In the school year of 2020–2021, a total of 8.4 million children and young people have attended schools of general education with the highest number of 1st grade beginners tracked in the last 14 years (Destatis, 2021c). However, the education system in the nation has been criticized sharply, especially after disappointing international test results. For instance, the PISA study results in 2000 has triggered the nation to make a reform in the educational system (Gruber, 2006). "Germany's children performed significantly below the OECD average, and a broad group was identified as 'functional illiterate', because their cognitive competences, reading and writing skills were inadequate for everyday needs" (Davoli & Entorf, 2018). After the reforms involving the standardization of curricula, increasing school autonomy and expanding and strengthening of educational content in pre-primary schools have led to an improvement in the recent PISA results published. According to OECD (2020, June) Germany ranked above average in reading, mathematics and science.

The Curriculum Development Process

The curricula in all states have been revised after the new strategy of digitalization which was introduced in 2016 by the standing conference (KMK). The prescribed curricula include guidelines on how to cover various topics of instruction, distribution of materials and various didactic approaches (KMK, 2019). In normal circumstances, if a state decides on revising a curriculum, the Ministry of Education and Cultural Affairs of the related state appoints a commission consisting of serving teachers, including heads and school inspectors as well as the research institute of the state. In addition, experts in the relevant disciplines from higher education are involved as well (Eurydice, n.d). Prior to being finalized and becoming generally accepted, the curricula are implemented on a trial basis. As soon as a new curriculum is introduced, the ministry organizes in-service training for teachers, while publishers are embarked on a revision or new edition of the textbook. The utilization of coursebooks as the primary material in education is prevalent among a majority of teachers.

The English Language Curriculum

Foreign language lessons are provided in primary schools in all states. In most states, compulsory foreign language lessons begin in grade 3; in three states pupils already begin in grade 1 (KMK, 2019). In *Hamburg* and *Rheinland-Pfalz* English lessons start to be taught at grade 1 and in *Brandenburg* in some cases at grade 1 or 2. In the year 2016, 80% of pupils at primary schools in half of the European Union countries learnt a compulsory foreign language, whereas in eight countries the rate was almost 100% (Kolb & Legutke, 2019). This demonstrates the significance designated to early bilingual education in Europe. In Germany, in the education year 2016–2017, around 7.4 million pupils learnt English which is equivalent to 86% of all pupils (Destatis, 2018).

The English language lessons are mainly based on competence-oriented curricula in line with the recommendations proposed by the standing conference (KMK) and are oriented towards the Common European Framework of Reference for Languages (KMK, 2019). In addition, between the years 2003 and 2004, all 16 states agreed on a declaration of formulations to achieve educational standards after finishing respectively primary and secondary school. For the English course, standards were formulated for the secondary schools *Hauptschule*, *Realschule* and upper secondary level *Gymnasium* (Köller, 2011).

As of grade 5 in all lower secondary schools, teaching foreign languages is a mandatory component of primary general education, and as of grade 7, it is a fundamental component of individual specialization. After passing to the lower secondary level, foreign language learning builds on sound competences acquired at the primary level and continuously expands on them (KMK, 2019).

Main Goals of the English Language Curriculum

The main goal of the English as a foreign language curriculum is the development of oral communicative competence with an emphasis on listening skills and audio-visual comprehension. The term 'communicative competence' was first introduced in detail by Hymes (1972). It emphasizes that speakers do not need to know only grammatical structures but also the norms of how to use the language and the appropriacy of social context. As also pointed out by Savignon (2018), spontaneous communication with all the grammar and pronunciation errors made during production is essential to develop communicative competence. Therefore, it attaches importance to a natural learning environment. Besides communicative competence, the curriculum emphasizes the structuring of a repertoire of verbal means to communicate, the development of reading and the recognition of typestyle. In addition, the development of reproductive writing, language awareness and intercultural competence are the core purposes. As language learners are seen as part of a global community in today's world, intercultural awareness and competence are enhanced.

Instructional Principles

The English language education in primary school is based on a natural language acquisition process. The learning context provides a holistic and authentic language experience. The methods applied include the activation of receptive and productive learning processes with an emphasis on learner-centred active learning. Thus, the program facilitates autonomy in learning and problem-solving and shifting from the traditional expository teaching to a more learner-based approach. It is of great importance to acquire these skills in primary education due to lifelong learning.

The primary language adopted in the classroom is the target language to provide sufficient language input. However, it is allowed to switch to the mother language if the transfer of the content has priority over the communicative realization. The curriculum also promotes phonetic and intonation via examples by supporting the perception and internalization of the sound system that triggers the recalling of speech patterns. Audio and visual comprehension is fostered by stories and audio samples which improve the internalization of the interpretation and imagination scope. The repetition, variation and spiral-formed curriculum support the learners' achievement and ability to express themselves in a flexible manner. The repetition of language functions in combination with the evolving repertoire is both the basis and goal of networking.

In terms of grammar, a linear grammatical progression is not provided in the curriculum. Based on a variety of language examples, rules should be deduced. The inductive learning approach is adopted in this program. Throughout the course, the students keep a portfolio of languages as an instrument for documenting the level of learning and learning processes. In this way, the pupils are stimulated and enabled to reflect on their own learning and document their intercultural experiences. The portfolio consists of a language passport, language biography and dossier. It is the teacher's job to provide advice to the students in creating their portfolios. The language portfolio, which was created in conjunction with the Common European Framework, is a personal document in which students can keep track of their intercultural experiences and language learning successes as well as set learning goals based on the skill descriptors of the CEFR (Council of Europe, n.d.).

The formative assessment promoted by the curriculum leads to an observation of the learning process. Due to individual differences of pupils, it is of vital importance to track the individual achievement of learners. Besides struggling to achieve a standard, it is obvious that the program values individual differences of pupils and their progress.

Objectives

Pupils are expected to achieve a number of objectives upon finishing grade 4. The primary school English language program of the federal state Saxony, for example, emphasizes listening, speaking, writing and reading skills. In addition, it aims to enhance intercultural competence and language awareness among children.

The pupils are expected to recognize the sound and rhythm of the target language and understand expressions describing their immediate environment. In addition, they are supposed to understand simple utterances on various topics.

Furthermore, they are expected to be able to engage in basic communication on familiar topics by using linguistic and non-linguistic means to express themselves.

In terms of reading, pupils will have gained first insights into individual words and phrases which have been saved in the sound image for comprehension by the time of finishing primary education.

The pupils will be able to engage in fill-in-the-blank writing activities. Moreover, they are expected to copy short authentic texts as they are able to recognize and assign individual words.

Another main objective is the acquisition of basic initial knowledge of the target countries to promote linguistic diversity as social normality. It is asserted that knowledge of other cultural backgrounds and their traditions fosters intercultural competence.

Finally, pupils are expected to develop an interest in languages and their diversity as they value the role of languages in social interaction.

An Overall Summary of the Primary School Curriculum

The primary school curriculum highlights oral competencies as one of the main objectives of early EFL education along with the acquisition of listening and audio-visual skills. Therefore, it neglects the writing skills which causes an imbalance between the four basic competencies. However, considering the onset age of English language learning, it matches the needs of the pupils. Due to the silent period in the language development process, receptive skills are fostered before productive skills.

The second primary goal of the program is to develop intercultural competence. It is aimed to provide information about the target language cultures. However, in a globalized world, language learning classes should also include activities that introduce cultures out of the target culture. It can be concluded that due to the extensive mobility between countries in Europe, high priority is given to raise intercultural awareness from an early age.

Conclusion

The decentralized and multi-track school system of Germany makes it quite complex to evaluate it in a unit form. The absence of nation-wide core standards leads to a broad power of decision for the boards of the individual states. Thus, the states and schools are able to adjust the program according to their needs. The curriculum provides a general framework with general objectives. The themes are not introduced in a specific sequence.

The English language program at primary level education is based on the 'communicative language learning approach'. It highlights listening and audio-visual comprehension. In view of this, it attaches attention to the silent period of learners. According to Drury (2013) during this period children need time to acclimatize to their new context and 'rehearse' the language silently to practise the utterances in 'private speech' until they feel comfortable using the language for communicative purposes. Another aspect of the program is that it highlights the importance of learning how to learn. The curriculum involves strategies for learning which support the language learning acquisition process. In addition, the portfolio provides an opportunity for learners to track, assess and reflect on their own learning which promotes the learning-to-learn process. The English language curriculum implicates twenty-first-century skills as well. One of the main objectives is to raise intercultural awareness among pupils. Due to the current situation of extensive interaction via physical or virtual means with other cultures, it enables the learners to become assets in the global community and fosters collaboration and relationships with other cultures. Besides, the use of strategies and media is also fostered which are essential skills of this century.

Finally, the implications drawn from the investigation of the primary school curriculum demonstrate that due to the complex structure and various school types, more emphasis should be given to collaboration with secondary schools to form a more holistic program as the transfer between schools tends to be compelling. Besides, the age of onset can be reduced to an earlier stage as the 'Critical Period Hypothesis' stresses the importance of an early start in language acquisition. The exposure to the English language should start at least in grade 1. Another strong feature of the program is that it provides a general framework for teachers that enables flexibility and room for adaptation.

According to the EF English Proficiency Index, which measures the English language proficiency rate among 112 countries, Germany has an excellent proficiency rate. Germany ranks 11th out of these 112 nations (Education First, 2021). The reason for the high level of proficiency in successful nations is associated with equal access to language education. Regardless of the socioeconomic status, the mobility and resources distributed and provided for all people equally lead to high achievement. It is used in the business sector as a lingua franca. However, the English language curricula for primary schools was first employed in the education year 2003 and 2004. Therefore, the rate of pupils who were educated with the current curriculum is not high. The long-term impact of the curriculum on business and work should be investigated later again.

Finally, it can be concluded that the current English language curriculum addresses contemporary approaches and innovations in language education. Germany is a country that sets an example for language learning policy in a decentralized system.

References

Auernheimer, G. (2005). The German education system: Dysfunctional for an immigration society. *European Education, 37*(4), 75–89.

Council of Europe. (n.d). *The European Language Portfolio.* https://www.coe.int/en/web/language-policy/european-language-portfolio

Davoli, M., & Entorf, H. (2018). *The PISA shock, socioeconomic inequality, and school reforms in Germany, IZA Policy Paper, No. 140.* Bonn: Institute of Labor Economics (IZA).

Destatis. (2018). *Schulen auf einem Blick.* Statistisches Bundesamt. https://www.destatis.de/DE/Themen/Gesellschaft-Umwelt/Bildung-Forschung-Kultur/Schulen/Publikationen/_publikationen-innen-schulen-blick.html

Destatis. (2021a). *Population by nationality and sex.* https://www.destatis.de/EN/Themes/Society-Environment/Population/Current-Population/Tables/liste-current-population.html;jsessionid= 160F1885988BC594210 37DC429611664.live712

Destatis. (2021b). *Bevölkerung und Demografie.* https://www.destatis.de/DE/Service/StatistikCampus/Datenreport/Downloads/datenreport-2021-kap-1.pdf?__blob=publicationFile

Destatis. (2021c). *Pressrelease #N 014 from 19 February 2021.*https://www.destatis.de/EN/Press/2021/02/PE21_N014_63.html

Drury, R. (2013). How silent is the 'Silent Period' for young bilinguals in early years settings in England? *European Early Childhood Education Research Journal, 21*(3), 380–391.

Education First. (2021). *EF English Proficiency Index: Eine Rangliste von 112 Ländern und Regionen nach Englischkenntnissen.* https://ef.com.tr/epi

Eurostat. (2021). *Population by country.* https://european-union.europa.eu/principles-countries-history/key-facts-and-figures/life-eu_en

Eurydice. (n.d). *Curriculum, subjects and number of hours.*https://eacea.ec.europa.eu/national-policies/eurydice

Gruber, K. H. (2006). *The German 'PISA-Shock': Some aspects of the extraordinary impact of the OECD's PISA study on the German education system.* Cross-national attraction in education: Accounts from England and Germany, 195–208.

Hymes, D. (1972). On Communicative competence. In J. B. Pride, & A. Holmes (Eds.), *Sociolinguistics: Selected readings.* Harmondsworth: Penguin.

Kolb, A., & Legutke, M. (2019). Englisch ab Klasse 1. Anmerkungen zu einer bildungspolitischen Diskussion. In A. Kolb, M. Legutke (Eds.), *Englisch ab*

Klasse 1-Grundlage für kontinuierliches Fremdsprachenlernen. Narr Francke Attempto Verlag.

KMK (Kultusministerkonferenz). (2019). *Das Bildungswesen in der Bundesrepublik Deutschland 2017/2018: Darstellung der Kompetenzen, Strukturen und bildungspolitischen Entwicklungen für den Informationsaustausch in Europa.* https://www.kmk.org/fileadmin/Dateien/pdf/Eurydice/Bildungswesen-dt-pdfs/dossier_de_ebook.pdf

Köller, O. (2011). Standardsetzung im Bildungssystem. In: Reinders H., Ditton H., Gräsel C., Gniewosz B. (Eds.), *Empirische Bildungsforschung.* VS Verlag für Sozialwissenschaften.

OECD. (2020, June). *Education Policy Outlook: Germany.* https://www.oecd.org/education/policy-outlook/country-profile-Germany-2020.pdf

Phillips, D. (Ed.). (1995). *Education in Germany: Tradition and reform in historical context* (1st ed.). Routledge. https://doi.org/10.4324/9780203355763

Pluntke, S. (2013). Bildungssystem der Bundesrepublik Deutschland. *In: Lehrrettungsassistent und Dozent im Rettungsdienst.* Springer, Berlin, Heidelberg.

Savignon, S. J. (2018). Communicative competence. *The TESOL encyclopedia of English language teaching,* 1–7.

Tuğçe Kılıç

Singapore: An Examination of English Language Curriculum

Lecturer, School of Foreign Languages, Istanbul University-Cerrahpasa,
Istanbul, Turkey
PhD student, English Language Education, Bahcesehir University,
Istanbul, Turkey

Abstract

Singapore has such diverse linguistical settings that it has four official languages: English, Malay, Tamil, and Mandarin Chinese. In Singapore, English has been taken as a national and international lingua franca (Pakir, 2010) and as a language that connects this island city-state to the rest of the world (Low & Pakir, 2018). To meet the country's needs, the English Language (EL) Curriculum and Pedagogy Review Committee (ELCPRC) was set up in September 2005 to revise and reshape the teaching and learning of English in Singapore schools (CA International, 2017). Having different school types based on the needs of the students, the curriculum was designed according to the needs of 21st-century pupils. Considering mastering skills such as critical thinking and problem-solving, it can be said that Singapore's EL curriculum sufficiently meets the needs of its students.

Keywords: EFL curriculum, Singapore, 21st-century skills

Introduction

Singapore has linguistically diverse settings that it has four official languages: English, Malay, Tamil, and Mandarin Chinese. As a result of colonization, inhabitants speak their mother tongues (Malay, Tamil, or Mandarin Chinese) and English. Due to globalization, teaching and learning English has gained importance. In Singapore, English has been taken as a national and international lingua franca (Pakir, 2010) and as a language that connects this island city-state to the rest of the world (Low & Pakir, 2018). To meet the students' needs and equip them with 21st-century competencies, they have adapted their 2010 curriculum in 2020 and have been following that to provide their students with quality education.

Examination

The English Language Curriculum and Pedagogy Review Committee (ELCPRC) was set up in September 2005 to revise and reshape the process of teaching and learning English in Singapore schools (CA International, 2017). In parallel, bilingualism and, in a broader sense, multilingualism has become the core of society since then (NUS, 2021).

Different school types meet every student's needs since, according to self-determination theory (SDT), students get motivated when they create relatedness with fellow students (Stolk et al., 2018). Thus, at the end of primary school, based on the results of the Primary School Leaving Examination (PSLE), pupils move on to the Specialized, Express, or Normal streams in secondary schools. The Normal stream is divided into the Normal Technical (NT) stream for the very weakest 15–20 % of pupils and the Normal Academic (NA) stream (Lee & Bathmaker, 2007). Specialized schools offer hands-on experience and practical learning. Express module includes an integrated program (IP), and it is for academically strong students (Figure 1).

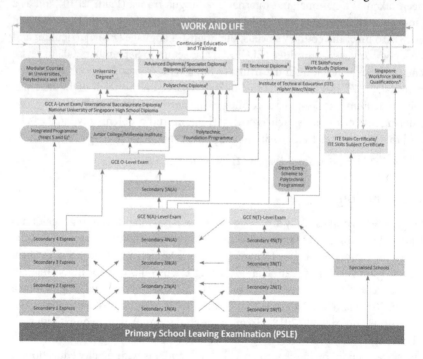

Figure 1 Singapore's Education System (MoE Curriculum, 2020)

According to the ELCPRC, the following are the four key points of a solid foundation in education: (1) A Curriculum for the Singapore Context; (2) Teacher Recruitment, Training, and Development; (3) Additional Support for Schools; and (4) Community Partnerships and Initiatives. Each type of school, namely NT, NA, Express, and Specialized, has its own curriculum. This chapter focuses on the English language curriculum of NA and Express schools which covers a broader area.

Before giving detailed information about the curriculum, one crucial thing that cannot go without saying is that the syllabi they use (English Language [EL] Syllabus, 2010) were built upon the previous one (EL Syllabus, 2001). Their motto is "building on the past and moving forward."

The current curriculum has three chapters: (1) Guiding Principles, (2) Areas of Language Learning, and (3) The Role of Language Teacher. The Ministry of Education (MoE) (2010) referred to the below topics:

- English in Singapore
- Desired Outcomes for EL Proficiency in Singapore
- Building on the Past
- Philosophy of Language Learning Underlying the EL Syllabus 2010
- Approach to EL Teaching in the EL Syllabus 2010
- Syllabus Aims
- Principles of EL Teaching and Learning
- Teaching Processes

The content makes it easy to understand that the curriculum was designed according to the needs of 21st-century pupils. In Singapore, students learn English and their native language, which they call Mother Tongue, in their curricula. English has different roles: It is the medium of instruction and a subject for primary and secondary school students (MoE, 2010). At the local level, the common language leads to socialization among the different communities. At the global level, English successfully allows Singaporeans to participate in a competitive economy (Suárez, 2005).

MoE (2010) also focuses on areas of language learning that are emphasized and delivered in an integrated and spirally. Unlike the segregated approach that teaches skills in isolation, the integrated-skill approach allows learners of English to experience authentic language and communicate fluently (Oxford, 2001). Furthermore, based on Bruner's cognitive theory (1960), a spiral curriculum makes the students repeatedly exposed to the same topic with increasing complexity during their education. Below are the skills focused on the EL curriculum:

- Listening and Viewing
- Reading and Viewing
- Speaking and Representing
- Writing and Representing
- Grammar
- Vocabulary

"To accommodate the increasingly diverse identities and experiences of Singaporeans," Wee (2013, p. 121) proposes that greater autonomy should be allowed in language choices. There are charts or checklists for every skill, which can be structured according to the needs and abilities of the students (Appendix A). This proves the learner-centered aspect of a curriculum with which 21st-century skills are easily transferred to diverse populations (Brown, 2003). In addition, coursebooks are used as the curriculum in classroom environments (Richards, 1998). There are MoE-approved publishers, and different books are used for different levels. Still, the checklists stay the same as teachers become developers of their own curriculum (MoE, 2010).

Finally, the role of the English teacher is discussed by MoE (2010). Teachers have different roles during teaching (Borg, 2006). In a VUCA world (an acronym for "volatility, uncertainty, complexity, and ambiguity"), it is exclusively essential to be flexible and adaptable. In the Singapore EL curriculum, teachers' first and foremost emphasis was making decisions about how to develop a language curriculum. Later comes the problem-solving skills so that they would match their way of teaching with their students' needs and development, creating safe and engaging classroom environments (Breen, 2017). The teaching processes to be applied are clearly defined in the curriculum (Appendix B).

Conclusion

In a world where we experience constant change, globalization is a term that refers to both uniformity and diversity worldwide (Burlacu & Gutu, 2018). Singapore is one of the pivotal locations of world trade, and it has a diverse and multicultural population from the whole world. On many occasions, English has been the lingua franca (Jenkins, 2009). Thus, it is only natural to have multilingual settings, and great importance has been given to language teaching. As this venture inherently requires mastering other skills such as critical thinking, problem-solving, etc., it can be said that Singapore's EL curriculum sufficiently meets the needs of its students. Furthermore, according to the flexibility that the curriculum gives its operators, namely teachers, we can infer that MoE (2010) pays attention to their teachers and invests greatly in teacher development.

References

Borg, S. (2006). *Teacher cognition and teacher education: Research and practice.* Continuum.

Breen, J. M. (2017). Leadership resilience in a VUCA world. *Visionary Leadership in a Turbulent World,* 39–58. doi: 10.1108/978-1-78714-242-820171003

Brown, K. L. (2003). From teacher-centered to learner-centered curriculum: Improving learning in diverse classrooms. *Education, 124*(1). Retrieved December 10, 2021, from https://go.gale.com/ps/i.do?id=GALE%7CA10 8911203&sid=googleScholar&v=2.1&it=r&linkaccess=abs&issn=00131 172&p=AONE&sw=w&userGroupName=anon%7Eef695ed9.

Bruner, J. S. (1960). *The process of education.* Harvard University Press.

Burlacu, S., & Gutu, C. (2018). Globalization – Pros and cons. *Quality – Access to Success, 19,* 122–125. Retrieved July 5, 2022.

Jenkins, J. (2009). English as a lingua franca: Interpretations and attitudes. *World Englishes, 28*(2), 200–207. https://doi.org/10.1111/j.1467-971x.2009.01582.x

Lee, R. N. F., & Bathmaker, A.-M. (2007). The Use of English Textbooks for Teaching English to 'Vocational' Students in Singapore Secondary Schools: A Survey of Teachers' Beliefs. *RELC Journal, 38*(3), 350–374. https://doi.org/ 10.1177/0033688207085852

Low, E. L., & Pakir, A. (2018). English in Singapore: Striking a new balance for future-readiness. *Asian Englishes, 20*(1), 41–53. https://doi.org/10.1080/13488 678.2018.1423455

Ministry of Education (MoE). (n.d.). Retrieved December 10, 2021, from https:// www.moe.gov.sg/.

Oxford, R. (2001). *Integrated Skills in the ESL/EFL Classroom.,* 1–7. Retrieved from www.eric.ed.gov.

Pakir, A. (2010). English as a lingua franca: Negotiating Singapore's English language education. *English in Singapore,* 261–279. https://doi.org/10.5790/ hongkong/9789888028436.003.0011

Report of the English Language Curriculum and Pedagogy Review. CA International College. (2017, April). Retrieved December 10, 2021, from https:// www.caic.com.sg/pdf/MOE%20English%20Review.pdf.

Richards, J. C. (1998). *Beyond training: Perspectives on language teacher education.* Cambridge University Press.

Singapore bilingual education: One policy, many interpretations. Fass.nus.edu.sg. (2021, September 7). Retrieved December 10, 2021, from https://fass.nus.edu. sg/srn/2021/09/07/singapore-bilingual-education-one-policy-many-interpre tations/.

Stolk, J. D., Jacobs, J., Girard, C., & Pudvan, L. (2018). Learners' needs satisfaction, classroom climate, and situational motivations: Evaluating self-determination theory in an engineering context. *2018 IEEE Frontiers in Education Conference (FIE)*. https://doi.org/10.1109/fie.2018.8658880

Suárez, S. L. (2005). Does English Rule? Language Instruction and Economic Strategies in Singapore, Ireland, and Puerto Rico. *Comparative Politics, 37*(4), 459. https://doi.org/10.2307/20072904

Wee, L. (2013). Governing English in Singapore: Some challenges for Singapore's language policy. In L. Wee, R. B. H. Goh, & L. Lim (Eds.), The politics of English: South Asia, Southeast Asia and the Asia Pacific (pp. 105–124).: John Benjamins Publishing Company.

Appendix A

ENGLISH LANGUAGE SYLLABUS 2010 (PRIMARY & SECONDARY)

Figure 1 Sample Chart/Checklist for Listening and Viewing Skills (MoE Curriculum, 2020)

Appendix B

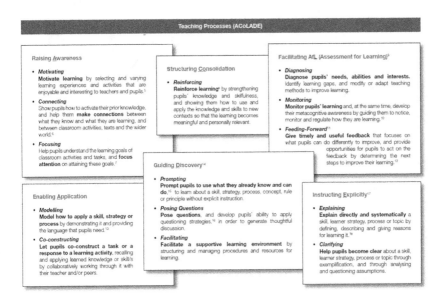

Figure 2 Teaching Processes that Are Applied Based on Students' Needs and Abilities (MoE Curriculum, 2020)

Tuba Kıvanç Contuk

English Language Curriculum in Slovakia

English Language Education, Bahçeşehir University, Istanbul, Turkey,
tuba.kivanccontuk@bahcesehir.edu.tr

Abstract

Being an indispensable communication tool, English has become popular as more and more people have been trying to learn this language. Thus, English language teaching and learning programs have gained importance throughout the world. This chapter aims to examine and reveal the strengths and weaknesses of the EFL curriculum of Slovakia. Starting from this point of view, it is also aimed to draw conclusions to contribute to the EFL curriculum and classroom applications in the world context.

Keywords: EFL curriculum, curriculum evaluation, Slovakia EFL curriculum, education system of Slovakia

Introduction

The advances in technology have enabled closer contact with people all around the world. People have had to develop a common language to communicate, do business, travel, and get educated in different parts of the world. To meet these aims, English serves as a lingua franca among people who do not share a common language (Jenkins, 2009; Seidlhofer, 2005). Being an indispensable communication tool, English has become popular as more and more people have been trying to learn this language. Thus, English language teaching and learning programs have gained importance throughout the world (Crystal, 2012). Therefore, the current chapter aims to report the guidelines of the EFL curriculum of Slovakia. From this perspective, it is also aimed to draw conclusions to contribute to the EFL curriculum and classroom applications in the world context.

The Education System of Slovakia

The education system of Slovakia consists of five main levels: pre-primary education, primary and lower secondary education, upper secondary education, higher education, and adult education (MoE, 2015). Pre-primary education is for children between 3 and 6. Primary and lower secondary education, on the other hand, refers to one unit and it lasts 9 years in total. Four years of this period is devoted to primary education. The rest of the duration is planned as lower secondary education. Primary and lower secondary education is conducted at the same schools. Upper secondary education starts at the age of 15. Students have three options to continue their education: general, vocational, and art schools. The duration of education at those schools varies from 2 to 8 years. Higher education encompasses three levels which are Bachelor's, Master's, and Ph.D. programs; universities and higher education institutions organize these programs. Finally, adults who want to extend their knowledge, re-qualify themselves or receive language education can start further education institutions, schools, and non-school organizations. Nurseries which provide education for children between 3 and 6 are not a part of the education system because The Ministry of Education, Science, Research and Sport of the Slovak Republic (MoE, 2015) is not responsible for this level. Municipalities, churches, or private entities can found nurseries (Eurydice, 2021).

The MoE in Slovakia develops the content, goal, and methods of education. Local, regional governance and municipalities provide funds, counseling services, and materials for the schools (Eurydice, 2021). Education is free of charge for all stages except adult education. Moreover, students are required to pay if they exceed their legal period for their studies. There are private schools as well, and students need to pay for these schools. Attending school for children between the ages of 6 and 16 is compulsory (MoE, 2015).

The Key Issues that Need Development in the Education System of Slovakia

According to the OECD's Education Policy Outlook (2015), The Republic of Slovakia should make the necessary improvements regarding equality in education, school dropouts, and the quality of vocational schools. Especially for students from disadvantaged groups such as Roma children, education is not accessible; consequently, their performances are generally low at school. Inequality and inaccessibility in education increase the risk of school dropouts. The needs for the labor market should be analyzed and more effective preparation programs in vocational schools should be constructed for students. To overcome the problems mentioned above, Slovakia introduced two acts: The School Act (National Institute for Education (NIE), 2007) and The New Act on VET (NIE, 2010). The School Act aims to decrease inequality and make the education system more accessible for disadvantaged groups. The New Act on VET, on the other hand, focuses on connecting education in vocational schools and the needs of the labor market.

Language Teaching System of Slovakia

Slovakia has experienced two major periods in language teaching. Before 1990, due to the communist regime, there were severe limitations on citizens' receiving foreign language education; traveling to other countries; and accessing radio broadcasts, movies, books, and magazines in a foreign language other than Russian. The sources such as textbooks, books, and audio or video materials were scarce (Enyedi & Medgyes, 1998). The books developed by the state were based on drills and other methods of grammar translation. Figure 1 presents the samples of textbooks before the 1990s (Kralova & Mala, 2018).

Figure 1 The Samples of Textbooks in the 1990s

However, after 1990, people in Slovakia had a chance to connect to the rest of the world, and the needs of the people and the country altered tremendously. As a result, the importance of learning Russian decreased and a number of different foreign languages such as English, German, Spanish, Italian, and French were offered to learners (Birova et al., 2017). With the dominance of English worldwide, teacher training programs for teaching English were established (Gadusova & Hartanska, 2002). In addition, after the abolishment of communism, the sources for teaching English were brought abroad and the institutions like The British Council and The Goethe Institut started teacher training programs in Slovakia (Kralova et al., 2014). Figure 2 presents the samples of coursebooks after the link was constructed with the rest of the world (Kralova & Mala, 2018).

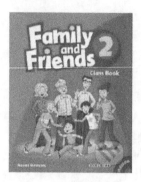  

Figure 2 The Samples of Coursebooks after the 1990s

The new era changed the rationale for teaching English. Cooperation with international associations led to a more systematic and innovative approach toward English teaching. In addition, the reform in 2007 made two foreign languages compulsory by the end of secondary education, with English having a special status (NIE, 2007). The new model also required the use of the Common European Framework of Reference for Languages (CEFR, 2001).

Today, English is taught at all stages of education. English instruction starts in the 3rd grade at state schools and it continues until the 9th grade with 3 hours of a week regarding primary and lower secondary education. In the 6th grade, students can select from various foreign languages as their second foreign language (Ciprianova et al., 2017). The coursebooks, on the other hand, are suggested by the MoE; however, the schools can decide their own books or add some extra materials such as workbooks. All the materials should be in line with the centralized curriculum and objectives of the CEFR. With the adoption of CEFR, the curriculum has now a tendency for a communicative approach and requires learners to communicate appropriately for the situation and cultural conventions. The MoE also aims to raise learners who can speak the given language and understand the way of life who speak that foreign language (MoE, 2015). In addition to state schools, there are also bilingual English-Slovak schools in which the medium of instruction is English after the extensive English teaching in the 1st year. Yet, these are private schools, and the number of these schools is very few at present. Learners continue to learn English at the tertiary level or at institutions which provide English instruction for the needs of the labor market or some international certification (Ciprianova et al., 2017).

Despite the improvements in English language teaching, Slovakia has some major issues that should be considered to construct a more effective system. Firstly, teacher qualification is an important problem and according to the report prepared by the MoE, teachers, especially the ones working at primary schools, lacked the necessary qualifications (NIE, 2010). Lower salaries and respect for teaching compared to other professions are accounted for one of the main reasons for the problem. Another main problem is the perceived low proficiency of the learners. The lack of contact with the foreign language and lack of support in foreign language education may be the reasons behind this incompetency (Strbova & Sarvajcova, 2021). The MoE has started some projects thanks to European Union (EU) funding to address the aforementioned problems (MoE, 2015).

Conclusion

In conclusion, the EFL curriculum of Slovakia is well structured and involves indispensable elements such as clear objectives according to grade levels and language skills, functions, sources, and intercultural dimensions. However, this structured and centralized curriculum gives autonomy to teachers and schools to some extent. Schools and teachers have a chance to select their coursebooks from a list given by the MoE. For lower secondary schools, evaluation is not based on national exams but on formative assessments the ways of which are decided by the teachers and administration are conducted through portfolios or oral performances. Furthermore, the curriculum encourages teachers to take decisions according to their contexts about the activities, strategies, and approaches so that students are not passive recipients of knowledge.

Thanks to recent improvements, it better addresses content and performance standards as well as the application of CEFR. In addition, there is an emphasis on sociolinguistic and communication competence because the main objective of the course is mentioned as gaining effective communication skills in speech and writing.

The EFL curriculum of Slovakia requires some improvements. Firstly, teacher qualification is an important issue as mentioned earlier. Consequently, the curriculum may also involve some guidelines regarding teacher development. The curriculum of Singapore, for example, addresses the issue of teacher development as a general objective (The MoE of Singapore, 2010). In addition, the roles of other stakeholders other than teachers and students are not stated in the curriculum. However, the research suggests that the school boards, parents, and the administration should contribute to the learning process of the students, and they have key roles in meeting the needs (Connelly, 2003; Danielson, 2007; Papay & Craft, 2016). In addition, technological tools or applications and the ways of integrating technology are not placed in the curriculum. In contrast to the curriculum of Slovakia, the EFL curriculum of the secondary schools in Turkey includes a specific part regarding the use of technology and blended learning and the advantages of integrating technology into classroom applications (The MoNE of Turkey, 2018). The necessity for integrating technology into education has also been stated by the International Society for Technology in Education (ISTE, 2007). According to ISTE (2007), students are expected to use their technological skills to solve problems and develop themselves in authentic and creative ways. These skills will enable them to live and learn effectively and productively in a global world. Thus, these issues need to be inserted into the curriculum as a basis and teachers can make adaptations to different learning/teaching contexts.

References

Birova, J., Vasbieva, D. G., & Masalimova, A. R. (2017). Communication in French foreign language learning by implementing the aspects of interculturality. *Communications, 19*(4), 95–104.

Ciprianova, E., Minasyan, S. V., & Ruda, O. (2017). English language education policies in east central Europe: The cases of Slovakia and Ukraine. *Cross- Cultural Studies: Education and Science, 2*(1), 49–66.

The Common European Framework of Reference for Languages. (2001). *Learning, teaching, assessment.* http://www.coe.int/t/dg4/linguistic/Source/Framework_EN.pdf.

Connelly, G. (2013). Redesigning evaluations to build capacity. *Principal, 92*(3), 52–65.

Crystal, D. (2012). *English as a global language.* Cambridge: Cambridge University Press.

Danielson, C. (2007). Enhancing professional practice: A framework for teaching (2nd ed.). ASCD.

Enyedi, A., & Medgyes, P. (1998). ELT in central and eastern Europe. *Language Teaching, 31*, 1–12.

Eurydice. (2021, January 29). National education systems: Slovakia. https://eacea.ec.europa.eu/national-policies/eurydice/content/slovakia_en.

Gadusova, Z., & Hartanska, J. (2002). Teaching English in Slovakia- Past, present, and future. *Revista de Filologia y Si Didactica, 25*, 225–280.

International Society for Technology in Education. (2007). *National educational technology standards for students*. https://www.iste.org/docs/pdfs/20-14_IST E_Standards-S_PDF.pdf.

Jenkins, J. (2009). English as a lingua franca: Interpretations and attitudes. *World Englishes, 28*(2), 200–207.

Kralova, Z., Bakay-Zahorska, M., & Cincibeaux, N. (2014). The historical background of the Slovak press in the USA. *Communications, 16*(3), 36–40.

Ministry of Education, Science, Research and Sport of the Slovak Republic. (2015, December 10). *Inovovaný štátny vzdelávací program pre základné školy* [The innovative state educational programme for primary schools]. https://www.minedu.sk/inovovany-svp-pre-zakladne-skoly/.

The National Institute for Education. (2007, December 15). Koncepcia vyučovania cudzích jazykov v základných a stredných školách [The conception of teaching foreign languages at primary and secondary schools]. http://www2.statpedu.sk/buxus/docs/predmety/kvcudzj.pdf.

The National Institute for Education. (2010, December 20). Perspektívy zavedenia povinného anglického jazyka v základných a stredných školách. Kvalifikovanosť učiteľov a dopad na kvalitu vzdelávania v oblasti cudzích jazykov [Perspectives of introducing English as a compulsory language in primary and secondary schools. The teachers' qualification and the impact on the quality of foreign language education]. https://www.statpedu.sk/ files/sk/o-organizacii/ projekty/rozvijanie-profesijnych-kompetencii/ zaverecna-sprava_projekt.pdf

OECD (2015), *Education Policy Outlook 2015: Making Reforms Happen*. OECD Publishing. http://dx.doi.org/10.1787/9789264225442-en.

Papay, J. P., & Kraft, M. A. (2016). The myth of the performance plateau. *Educational Leadership, 73*(8), 36–41.

Seidlhofer, B. (2005). English as a lingua franca. *ELT Journal, 59*(4), 339–341.

Singapore Ministry of Education. (2010). *English language syllabus 2010: Primary & secondary*. https://www.moe.gov.sg/-/media/files/primary/english-primary-secondary-express-normal-academic.pdf.

Srtbova, M., & Sarvajcova, M. (2021). Necessity of improvement of foreign language teaching in the Slovak Republic. *Journal of Education Culture and Society, 2*, 251–263. doi:10.15503.jecs2021.2.251.263.

Turkey Ministry of National Education. (2018). Ortaöğretim İngilizce dersi öğretim programı. https://mufredat.meb.gov.tr/ProgramDetay.aspx?PID=342.

Merve Nur Özet

A Closer Look into Estonian English Language Curriculum

English Language Education, Bahçeşehir University, Istanbul, Turkey,
mervenur.ozet@bahcesehir.edu.tr

Abstract

Estonia is one of the post-Soviet countries where educational policies were reshaped several times to abandon centralized curricular policies. Exploration of curriculum policies in Estonia is a good opportunity to contextualize the discussions of centralization versus decentralization of national curricula. In an effort to recover from the prescriptive, top-down-imposed and centralized education policies of the Soviet era, Estonia oriented towards integrating western educational principles into their curriculum at all levels. It is easy to observe a transition process from the implementation of fully centralized educational policies to creating a more decentralized educational system. The current study will focus on providing a general overview of educational practices in Estonia as well as elaborating on its unique historical status and its reflections on curricular decisions.

Keywords: Estonia, English language curriculum, English language teaching, English as a foreign language

Introduction

The current chapter focuses on providing a general overview of educational practices in Estonia as well as elaborating on its unique historical status and its reflections on curricular decisions. Examination of curriculum policies in Estonia is a good opportunity to contextualize the discussions of centralization versus decentralization of national curriculums. In an effort to recover from the prescriptive, top-down-imposed and centralized education policies of the Soviet Era, Estonia oriented towards integrating western educational principles into their curriculum at all levels (Errs, 2018, Mikser, Kärner & Krull, 2016, Rouk, 2016, Siiner, 2014). It is easy to observe a transition process from the implementation of fully centralized educational policies to creating a more decentralized educational system. This transition process and its implications for stakeholders are worthwhile to study.

A General Look at Language Education System in Estonia

Children begin to have schooling experience at 18 months of age, spanning to 6 years of age, with preschool education, which is not mandatory. Mandatory education is composed of primary education and secondary education. Students can choose to have a basic education that is composed of three stages. Stage 1 covers grades 1–3, Stage 2 covers grades 4–6, and Stage 3 covers grades 7–9. The graduation requirement for basic schools is passing the Estonian language Exam, a second language exam, a Mathematics exam, and completing a performance-based assignment. Upon graduation from basic education, students have three choices which are practicing an occupation, continuing in vocational secondary school, and being educated in an upper secondary school. National education for basic education includes the following subjects: Language and Literature, Foreign Languages, Mathematics, Natural Science, Social Studies, Art Subjects, Technology, Physical education, Religious studies, Informatics, Career education, and Entrepreneurship studies (Ministry of Education and Research, https://www.hm.ee/en/activities/pre-school-basic-and-secondary-education).

These subjects are given to provide general descriptions of required competences that will guide the organization of courses. The subjects are guidelines to create specific courses based on the expected learning outcomes. To illustrate, competence in social studies entails "ability to understand the causes and effects of changes in society; knowledge of and respect for human rights and democracy; knowledge of civil rights and responsibilities and ability to behave accordingly" (Ministry of Estonian Education – MEE, 2014a, p. 2), and the curriculum of social studies lessons that are History, Civics and citizenship education, Personal, social and health education, and Religious studies can be shaped based on the given learning objective (MEE, 2014b).

General secondary education enables students to continue their studies at a university or transfer to a vocational school. The Curriculum of General secondary education is composed of mandatory and selective courses that students need to pass at least 96 of them. The graduation requirement is passing of Estonian language exam, state exam, a second language exam, upper secondary school exam, and completing a project assignment (MEE, 2014b). General provisions for national education of secondary education include guidelines subsumed under the subjects of language and literature, foreign languages, mathematics, natural science, social studies, art subjects, physical education, religious studies, national defense, economic and business studies, philosophy, career education, and bases of inquiry.

It is necessary to give brief information about vocational educational schools to highlight the efforts of the Ministry of Education to meet the demands of job markets in giving high-quality Vocational Education Teaching (VET) (Pauline, Simon, Anthony & Benedicte, 2019). With the approval of the Vocational Education Institutions Law, vocational education was divided into two levels: vocational secondary education and vocational higher education. Work-Based Learning (WBL) is given a specific focus in VET curriculum and 50 % of courses are expected to draw on WBL in the design of course content. WBL involves gaining work-related experience, experiencing work-place atmosphere, and gaining soft skills of effective customer communication and support (Musset, Mann & Field, Bergseng, 2019). Strong emphasis on WBL and efforts to update the curriculum and structure of vocational high schools mainly is due to the urgent demand for highly skilled workers. The New Qualification system of VET is created under the consultancy of employers, which is a significant step to expand the overlap between needed skills and acquired skills.

Some important points to be made regarding the subjects of national curriculum and assessment system are a strong emphasis on the national language and promotion of it along with an effort to create multilingual citizens. Additionally, a striking finding is that vocational high schools benefit greatly from the localization of education as the connection between theory and practice becomes stronger with the efforts to bridge the gap between the expected competences of the job market and the curricular objectives of vocational schools.

Language Policies and Language Education in Estonia

Before moving on to language policies, it would be insightful to give some background on the structure of general curriculum. Estonian curriculum is a compartmentalized curriculum that can be examined in two parts of National Curriculum (NC) and Subject Curriculum (SC) (Erss, Mikser, Löfström, Ugaste, Rouk, & Jaani, 2014). NC is a set of guidelines that are concerned with promoting "humanistic and democratic values, equal educational opportunities, openness, social and economic relevance, and the balance between the Estonian national identity, Europeanization and internationalization" (MEE, 2014b). Such comprehensiveness is the content of the NC that it even includes "that regional needs, the needs of school staff, parents and pupils, and the resources to be used" (MEE, 2014a). SC, the subject syllabi, derives its foundations regarding the outcomes, teaching methods, and modes of delivery from NC to create subject specifications for each course (Mikser, Kärner & Krull, 2016).

Effects of the Soviet legacy on Estonian language education have persisted to this day as the Soviet era brought about huge changes, even redefining the status of the Estonian language as being a secondary language. Therefore, restoring of the official status of Estonian as being the main medium of interaction in the public and social sphere is at the core of all language policies (Kestere, Sarv & Stonkuviene, 2020; Siiner, 2014). Estonia witnessed the re-structuring of its language and culture during the Soviet period (from 1940 to 1989), which is the result of Soviet rule's decision to use Russian as an official language in all Soviet countries (Siiner, 2014). Parallel school system in Estonia has its roots in Russian only language policy, dating back to the times of Soviet rule.

Parallel school system refers to two types of schools that are Estonian-medium schools and Russian-medium schools. Estonian population consists of citizens from all the former soviet citizens, thereby creating a linguistically diverse population. However, the second dominant linguistic group is Russians that led to the creation of this two-tiered educational system. To ensure the smooth cultural and linguistic integration of Russian-speaking population as well as other immigrants, and help the Estonian language regain its former status, Estonia went through a "restoration and integration" process (Siiner, 2014, p. 609).

Restoration involved successful "language socialization" of immigrant kids and Russian speakers through integrating obligatory Estonian language courses into the curriculum and assessing the competences with state-based language examinations (Siiner, 2014, p. 609). In Russian-medium schools, it is mandatory for students to choose Estonian as the second language (Language A along with English). Although the effectiveness of Estonian language education is criticized due to lack of resources, teachers, and materials, it might be viewed as a significant step to eliminate communication breakdowns and promote the Estonian language to the status of the National language.

Integration policy is created in line with the educational principles of the European Council to keep pace with the western ideals of multilingualism and universal citizenship. Membership in the European Union (EU) in 2004 marked the beginning of the efforts to gain the status of a European state (Rouk, 2013). An increased mobility due to trade relations is what characterizes the process of from being a candidate to a member state (1997–2004). To meet the linguistic needs arising from increased mobility, language policies were aligned with recommendations given in language policy documents of the Council of Europe.

To this end, two language courses are added to the general education curriculum. The main aim is to create plurilingual citizens with a B2 level of proficiency in Language A, and B1 level of competence in language B (Raud, 2008). English is taught as Language A starting form 2nd grade with 2–3 hours of instruction per week. Language B is determined by the interplay of various factors that are "The availability of the teacher, the preferences of children and their parents" (Raud, 2008, p. 42).

In line with the competence descriptors stated by the Common European Framework of References (CEFR), the Upper Secondary Education Language curriculum document advised the integration of general competences into language studies. "Forming general competencies" through language education involves tapping into the cultural and value competence, social and citizenship competence, and self-awareness competence, learning to learn competence, communication competence, entrepreneurial competence mathematics, natural sciences, and technological competence (MEE, 2014b). To be entitled as multilingual European citizens, students need to gain all sorts of social and communicative competences. In this regard, curriculum document advised the contextualization of language input in relation to various competences.

Another significant feature of language curriculum is the holistic approach to language competence since intercultural competence is also aimed to be improved along with language skills. Language competence involves cultivating respect and tolerance towards other cultures in students, and performance-based descriptors of learning objectives are given below:

Learning objectives
1) have language acquire language proficiency at a level that enables them to act independently in an authentic foreign language environment;
2) understand and value the similarities and differences of their own and other cultures.
3) communicate with the speakers of the target language by considering their cultural norms; 4) are able to continue their studies in a foreign language, take part in varied international projects and use foreign languages in an international working environment;
5) analyze their knowledge and skills and strengths and weaknesses and have the motivation and acquire the skills necessary for lifelong learning (MEE, 2014b, p. 14).

To conclude, changes in language policies regarding the nationalization of education as well as the adoption of multiculturalism-oriented language policies given above are the results of attempts to adopt "Western (more British-American) curricular thinking and tradition," and these changes are significant elements of the liberalization process pioneered by Gorbachov (Rouk, 2013, p. 86).

From Centralization to Decentralization

Soviet countries have highly unitary and standardized teaching programs that function as ideological tools to create communist citizens (Erss, 2018; Zajda, 1988). The main aim of schooling can be summed as the promotion of "Marxist-Leninist ethics and moral codes" that later formed the basis of moral education, a striking component of Soviet-era curriculums (Zajda, 1988, p. 389). From 1945 to 1988, till the fall of the Soviet Union, communist propaganda together with its reflections on teaching practices was an important aspect of Soviet pedagogy. Soviet-type school uniforms, mandatory moral education, the teaching of history from the Soviet perspective, and use of Soviet-approved teaching materials are some of the defining features of formal education in Soviet Union countries.

It is easy to grasp the power of central authority regarding the curricular studies by looking at the content, and in the first place, the emergence of Moral education as being the core course in the curriculum of secondary school. Below is the content of moral education that was believed to be optimal to teach at the ages of 10–17.

(1) Formation of moral traits which determine the relationship of man towards society.
(2) Formation of a communist attitude towards labour.
(3) Formation of an ethical (moral) attitude towards people.
(4) Formation of moral attitudes of people towards their own behaviour.
(5) Cultivation of moral values within one's family. (Zajda, 1988, p. 392)

Although there was an obligation to teach all the courses on the background of the aforementioned moral education and communist ideology, there was a tendency to implement the hidden curriculum. This tendency can be seen as a reaction, in the form of a silent protest, towards the lack of any teacher agency in the designation and implementation of the curriculum. Other Baltic countries had their own hidden curriculum in teaching. Teachers reported using some non-verbal cues (showing discontent), omission of some parts, and resistance to represent national symbols in their clothes. These slight disobediences were later perceived as attempts to create and practice a hidden curriculum by teachers (Kreitzberg, 1995).

The shift from the use of a centralized curriculum to the decentralization of curriculum was remarkably abrupt and unexpected as it is the case in reforms in economy, politics, and ideology of the Soviet bloc. The fall Soviet Union transformed the educational policies due to the emergence of "a new liberal market state with neoliberal values and decentralized education system" (Erss, 2018, p.

239). There was a detachment from the unitary, standardized, and top-down imposed educational policies to search for new educational policies that would be in line with expectations of newly structured political ideology (Tuul, Mikser, Neudorf, & Ugaste, 2015). These efforts resulted in three different curriculum reforms in 1989, 1997, and 2011 that mainly aimed to give a greater agency to teachers and align the curriculum with European educational practices.

Decentralization of Curriculum and Teacher Autonomy

Pedagogical Research Institute, Curriculum Laboratory of Tallinn Pedagogical University, and the Center of Educational Planning of Estonia are official bodies responsible for curriculum design and innovation (Rouk, 2013). Initiatives of these institutions to enhance the curriculum ownership of the teachers have aimed to give greater responsibilities to teachers. Expert opinions on the local context and its reflections on the curriculum are highly needed to answer the regional educational needs of the students. Additionally, ownership of the curriculum was conceived to be a significant step in the lifelong engagement of professional development. To this end, the main responsibility of teachers was determined to be one of the developers of a school curriculum based on the framework of the national curriculum, with the aim of specifying the learning outcomes at the class level, adding locally relevant and profile-related content, and determining the learning processes and assessment (Errs, 2018).

Not only at a school level but also a state level ownership of curriculum by teachers was aimed to be achieved and a major step was taken to integrate teachers in the curriculum-making process. The first step in curriculum reform of 1997 involved inviting teachers to curriculum compilation studies together with other stakeholders in education (Erss, Mikser, Löfström, Ugaste, Rouk, & Jaani, 2014, Rouk, 2013, Tuul et al., 2015). After the compilation of NC, teachers were expected to create their SC based on the general guidelines provided by NC.

How promising it seems though, teacher ownership of curriculum has become subject to considerable debate among teachers (Mikser et al., 2016; Errs, 2018). Teachers were taken by surprise at the very beginning of the curriculum-making process as it meant an abrupt shift of responsibility for teachers. Teachers expressed their concerns various times regarding the unavailability of resources to draw on (Mikser et al., 2016), poor professional credibility (Mikser et al., 2016; Tuul et al., 2016), and high expectations of official bodies (Tuul et al., 2016, Kestere, 2020). Particularly, the studies conducted with novice teachers of the transformation process indicated that teachers were not prepared to create their own subject syllabus due to lacking any prior knowledge of curriculum development.

They voiced their concerns regarding the lack of any curriculum design courses in teacher education departments (Mikser et al., 2016)

In addition to concerns regarding having no prior experience, teachers were also concerned about the high expectations of NC in terms of learning object-ives to be covered in SC. It was a big hindrance for teachers to focus on their selection of content and subject as NC provides a long list of learning object-ives to be included in the subject syllabus (Tuul et al., 2015). Teachers reported feeling overwhelmed sometimes due to creating a SC based on this loaded NC (Mikser et al., 2016; Tuul et al., 2015). Another concern is that NC guidelines do not take into classroom realities in relation to the availability of resources thereby expanding the gap between learning objectives and classroom practice (Errs, 2018). Teachers reported having great difficulty in meeting the objectives of art and sports lesson.

Conclusion

A closer look at the education system and curricular reforms in Estonia gives greater insights into the age-old debate of centralization versus decentralization and teacher ownership of the curriculum. As a matter of fact, efforts to decen-tralize the curriculum with a specific aim to account for regional and local factors and giving agency to local actors in curriculum design yielded some conflicting results. To the teachers, localization attempts did not fully serve the purpose of creating a regional or local SC as NC determines the learning outcomes and objectives to be covered in SC. In this regard, it might be said that the Situational Analysis and Needs Analysis parts of the curriculum were disregarded due to the abruptness of the shift to a new approach in curriculum making.

Another issue to be raised is the unwillingness of teachers to create their own teaching syllabus and their inefficiency beliefs regarding curriculum design. As part of the efforts to ensure teacher ownership curriculum, teachers were invited to create their own subject syllabus. Studies indicated that enhanced teacher agency contributed to their professional development. However, the lack of a mediator between teachers and other stakeholders to support teachers in profes-sional development activities hindered the smooth transition to the new system. This hindrance indicated the significance of professional development activities and having strong communication among all parties during the times of any kind of curriculum reform. It is significant to collaborate with the teacher in each step of the curriculum design.

References

Erss, M. (2018). 'Complete freedom to choose within limits'–teachers' views of curricular autonomy, agency and control in Estonia, Finland and Germany. *The Curriculum Journal, 29*(2), 238–256.

Erss, M., Mikser, R., Löfström, E., Ugaste, A., Rouk, V., & Jaani, J. (2014). Teachers' views of curriculum policy: The case of Estonia. *British Journal of Educational Studies, 62*(4), 393–411.

Kestere, I., Sarv, E. S., & Stonkuviene, I. (2020). Estonian Curriculum Becoming Independent. In *Pedagogy and Educational Sciences in the Post-Soviet Baltic States, 1990–2004: Changes and Challenges.* 84–101.

Kreitzberg, P. (1995). *The legitimation of educational aims: Paradigms and metaphors.* Sweden: Lund University.

Mikser, R., Kärner, A., & Krull, E. (2016). Enhancing teachers' curriculum ownership via teacher engagement in state-based curriculum-making: the Estonian case. *Journal of Curriculum Studies, 48*(6), 833–855.

Ministry of Estonian Education (MEE). (2014a). National Curriculum for Upper Secondary Schools, *Appendix 2 of Regulation No 2 of the Government of the Republic of 6 January 2011.* Available at https://www.hm.ee/en/national-curricula-2014

Ministry of Estonian Education (MEE). (2014b). National Curriculum for Upper Secondary Schools, *Appendix 5 of Regulation No 1 of the Government of the Republic of 6 January 2011.* Available at https://www.hm.ee/en/national-curricula-2014

Musset, P., Field, S., Mann, A., & Bergseng, B. (2019). *Vocational education and training in Estonia.* OECD Publishing. France.

Pauline, M., Simon, F., Anthony, M., & Benedicte, B. (2019). OECD reviews of vocational education and training *vocational education and training in Estonia.* OECD Publishing.

Raud, N. (2008). Foreign language education at the primary level in Estonia. In *Seminar Papers on Early Foreign Language Education* (p. 37– 44). Finland.

Rouk, V. (2016). From Times of Transition to Adaptation: Background and Theoretical Approach to the Curriculum Reform in Estonia 1987–1996. *Bulgarian Comparative Education Society.*

Siiner, M. (2014). Decentralisation and language policy: Local municipalities' role in language education policies. Insights from Denmark and Estonia. *Journal of Multilingual and Multicultural Development, 35*(6), 603–617.

Tuul, M., Mikser, R., Neudorf, E., & Ugaste, A. (2015). Estonian preschool teachers' aspirations for curricular autonomy–the gap between an ideal and professional practice. *Early Child Development and Care, 185*(11–12), 1845–1861.

Zajda, J. (1988). The moral curriculum in the Soviet school. *Comparative education, 24*(3), 389–404.

Rumeysa Yücel

National English Program in Basic Education of Mexico

English Language Education, Bahçeşehir University, Istanbul, Turkey,
rumeysa.yucel@bahcesehir.edu.tr

Abstract

This chapter aims to reflect the picture of implementations of English language education in primary school and examine and evaluate features of the curriculum in Mexico. The education system is governed by two parties which are central and regional authorities. There 32 states in Mexico and education services and their implementation norms change from state to state. Basic and teacher education was decentralized in 1992 within the scope of modernization of national basic education. The English curriculum has gone through many changes over years depending on the changes of the governments and their different educational policy views, leading to turmoil in the schools.

Keywords: Primary education, language curriculum, Mexico

Introduction

Mexico is in Central America and it hosts 128.933 million people. The rate of dependent population (0–14 ages) is 25.84 % in 2020 according to data from the United Nations. Primary, secondary, and tertiary level of education enrolment rates are orderly 95 %, 80.6 %, and 42.8 % based on 2019 data from UNESCO. It is interesting that female enrolment in secondary and tertiary levels of education is higher than their male peers. Also, the rate of education enrolment for ages between 15 and 19 is the lowest rate among OECD and partner countries depending on the data of OECD 2019.

The education system is governed by two parties which are central and regional authorities. There are 32 states in Mexico and education services and their implementation norms change from state to state. Basic and teacher education began to be decentralized in 1992 within the scope of modernization of national basic education. The Mexican Secretariat of Public Education (Secretaría de Educación Pública, SEP), which is a federal government authority with Cabinet representation, is responsible for control and implementation of national educational policy and school standards and it shares this responsibility with each state's ministry of education (British Council, 2015).

According to Zhizhko (2015), modern Mexican education system consists of basic education (preschool, primary school, and secondary school), preparatory school, higher education, and postgraduate education. Compulsory education entails ages between 6 and 15 which are primary school (age category 6–12 years) and junior secondary school (age category 12–15 years). The language of education is Spanish and education in public schools is free of charge for all levels (The Dutch Organization for Internationalization in Education, 2015).

English Language Education in Public Primary School

Teaching English in public schools was limited to middle and high school levels until the early 1990s. With the pressure of international organizations and the idea that starting to learn a language at early age facilitates permanent learning, English lessons began to be incorporated into primary schools' curricula (Romero & Sayer, 2016). However, English was not integrated subsequently into primary school curricula in all states. In the beginning, English lessons were implemented in 5 states and then the number increased to 13 states between the years 2000 and 2003. Within the following years, the number was increased to 22 states and then expanded to all states in orderly 2010 and 2012 (SEP 2011; Romero & Sayer, 2016).

The National English Program in Basic Education

To provide uniformity of various English programs from different levels, National English Program in Basic Education (NEPBE in English, or PNIEB in Spanish) was created and implemented in the 2009–2010 school year as a pilot study, and it was tuned and rearranged depending on the feedbacks and was expanded in all states by 2012. NEPBE had some drawbacks in terms of being inconsistent with the locally developed curriculum by teachers in each state (Sayer, 2015; Romero & Sayer, 2016).

In 2015, NEPBE was changed into the National English Program; PRONI (Programa Nacional de Inglés in Spanish) by the Federal Government (Romero & Sayer, 2016). This program is not different from NEPBE in terms of content, but it aims to develop materials for teaching and learning English and provide their distribution to all states and improve teacher education with international academic certifications until 2016 (SEP, 2015). Also, in the process of implementing PRONI in schools, the state government must sign an agreement with the federal government. A recent change was conducted in 2020 in PRONI. It targets to facilitate technology use in English lessons (SEGOB, 2020).

NEPBE 2012

NEPBE 2012 is piloted and used in all states now contrary to its updated versions. The purpose of NEPBE 2012 is to increase the quality of education thus raising well-educated nations. It also aims to develop 21st-century competencies of learners with recent pedagogical approaches and teaching methods by renovating syllabus contents (SEP, 2012).

According to NEPBE 2012, basic education is divided into three cycles: Cycle 1 entails preschool and 1st and 2nd grade of primary school, Cycle 2 includes third and 4th grade, and lastly Cycle 3 involves 5th and 6th grade.

Contents are divided into two categories which are 'Social practices of the language' and 'specific competencies with the language'. In this sense, through the three cycles, it is expected to develop students' problem-solving skills and organization of thoughts and speech in English as well as using English in everyday and unexpected situations. Beyond that, each cycle has its own aims.

English lessons are 300 hours for each class (first and second class of primary education), yet it decreases by 200 hours per fourth and fifth classes. From 1st to 6th grade, lessons are arranged as 50-minute sessions and at the end of primary school, students are expected to reach A2 level based CEFR and it corresponds to Cycle 3 in CENNI (Certificación Nacional de Nivel de Idioma; National certifications of language level adopted from CEFR) (NEPBE, 2012).

Cycle 2 entails 3rd and 4th grades. At the end of this cycle, students are expected to

- Clarify wishes and opinions and use common situations to do so.
- Recognize elementary directions, facts, and adverts.
- Recognize fundamental facets of vocabulary and pronunciation utilized in circumstances relevant to daily living.
- Use terms to discuss personal characteristics and requirements.
- React in various linguistic and nonlinguistic ways to spoken and written language.
- Use a variety of approaches to find solutions to common issues and to research specific subjects.
- Recognize the connections and contrasts between the expressions of their own cultures and those of the English language.
- Make fundamental social connections using their verbal skills (NEPBE, 2012).

According to Aziz et al. (2018), there should be parallelism among the objectives, aims, and teaching content of the curriculum. In that sense, the above-mentioned aims are parallel with the objectives in social practices of language which constitute three subtracts (familiar and community environment, literary and ludic environment, academic and educational environment) and specific competencies (see Appendix). For example, to reach the aim of 'Establishing basic social contact using their linguistic repertoire', students are anticipated to get through the objectives of social practices of the language. 'Offer and receive information about oneself and acquaintances' in the familiar community environment part and 'read narrative texts and recognize cultural expressions from English-speaking countries' in the literary and ludic environment part are the examples. Then they 'formulate and answer questions to find information about a specific topic' in the academic and educational environment part.

In short, the overall aim of NEPBE 2012 is to help students gain 21st-century skills which also include digital literacy. There are objectives in the familiar and community environment part within Cycle 2 named 'interpret the message in the advertisement' and 'displaying sequence of experiment' in the unit plan. In these activities, students can prepare graphs or search for similar examples on the internet. However, according to a report by the National Institute for the Evaluation of Education (INEE) (2018), more than 60 % of public schools don't have the internet and 4.9 % don't have electricity.

Program Implementation

According to NEPBE 2012, English lessons are planned as 50-minute sessions, but in some areas, English lessons are not implemented in a regular way because of the lack of English teachers. They try to implement English lessons three times a week with 45-minute sessions.

As for assessment, formative assessment, which evaluates students' performance during the whole semester with portfolios, teacher observation, and classroom discussions to get deeper insights into what students know or learn (Boston, 2002), is conducted by the teachers (NEPBE, 2012). Another assessment technique is self-evaluation which is intended to help students evaluate their performance on electronic forms.

Conclusion

In this chapter, NEPBE 2012 was examined by putting Cycle 2 as part of the curriculum to the center. The English curriculum has gone through many changes over years depending on the changes of the governments and their different educational policy views, leading to turmoil in the schools. Firstly, in the current situation, NEPBE 2012 is the only pilot curriculum applied in all states, yet the new one PRONI 2020 is starting to be applied in a few states as well. Secondly, the idea of unification of the program is beneficial to provide equity among the students. However, as stated by Sayer (2015), socioeconomic situations in Mexico are different from state to state. In this sense, for example, integrating technology into education is not a practical aim for all states. At the broader level, even most of the schools neither have electricity nor computers. Furthermore, sustainable economic sources provided by the government are not the same for all states. Thirdly, formative assessment can be fruitful in language classrooms, and it overlaps the objectives of Cycle 2 as well. Nevertheless, primary schools suffer from permanent English teachers. In this case, it is becoming hard and nonrealistic to conduct a formative assessment with a wide range of different temporary teachers during the whole semester. Lastly, there are no specific obligatory English course books, and schools or states are required to prepare their own didactic materials based on the aims and objectives of NEPBE 2012. If locally prepared materials can be evaluated by professional authorities and their content can be prepared for meeting the curriculum aim, the teaching process will be more efficient.

References

Aziz, S., Mahmood, M., & Rehman, Z. (2018). Implementation of CIPP model for quality evaluation at school level: A case study. *Journal of Education and Educational Development, 5*(1), 189–206.

Boston, C. (2002). The concept of formative assessment. *Practical Assessment, Research, and Evaluation, 8*(1), 9.

British Council (2015). *"English in Mexico: An examination of policy, perceptions and influencing factors".* https://www.teachingenglish.org.uk/sites/teacheng/files/English%20in%20Mexico.pdf

Cameron, L. (2003). Challenges for ELT from the expansion in teaching children. *ELT journal, 57*(2), 105–112.

National Institute for the Evaluation of Education (INEE). (2018). "Políticas para fortalecer la infraestructura escolar en México". https://www.inee.edu.mx/wp-content/uploads/2018/12/documento5-infraestructura.pdf

Nuffic (2015). *Education system Mexico described and compared with the Dutch system.* https://www.nuffic.nl/sites/default/files/2020-08/education-system-mexico.pdf

OECD (2013)."Education Policy Outlook Mexico ". https://www.oecd.org/mex ico/EDUCATION%20POLICY%20OUTLOOK%20MEXICO_EN.pdf

OECD Data. Mexico. https://data.oecd.org/mexico.htm

Romero, J. L. R., & Sayer, P. (2016). The teaching of English in public primary schools in Mexico: More heat than light?. *Archivos Analíticos de Políticas Educativas= Education Policy Analysis Archives, 24*(1), 92.

Sayer, P. (2015). Expanding global language education in public primary schools: The national English programme in Mexico. *Language, Culture and Curriculum, 28*(3), 257–275.

Secretaria de Educación Pública (SEP). (2011). Acuerdo 592, por el que se establece la articulación de la educación básica. Retrieved February 1, 2016, from: http://basica.sep.gob.mx/seb2010/pdf/destacado/Acuerdo_592.pdf.

Secretaría de Educación Pública (SEP). (2012). "The National English Program in Basic Education". https://www.gob.mx/sep/documentos/programa-ingles-primaria?state=published

Secretaría de Educación Pública (SEP). (2015). Principales Cifras del Sistema Educativo Nacional 2014–2015.

Secretariat of Public Education (Mexico) (SEP). https://fundit.fr/en/institutions/ secretariat-public-education-mexico-sep.

SEGOB (2020)." *Operación del Programa Nacional de Inglés para el ejercicio fiscal 2021*". https://www.dof.gob.mx/nota_detalle.php?codigo=5609 166&fecha=29/12/2020.

UNESCO Institute for Statics. Mexico. http://uis.unesco.org/en/country/mx.

Zhizhko, E. (2015). The background and development of Mexican educational system: The main features. *Labor et Educatio*, Vol. 3, 93–101.

Appendix

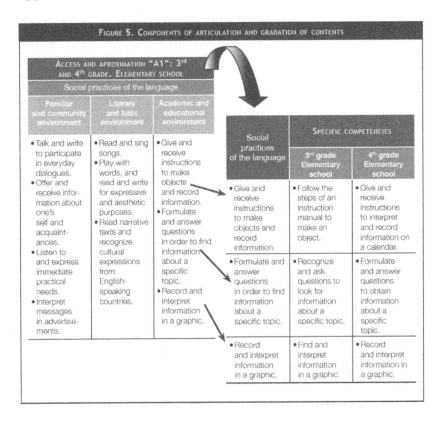

Figure 1 Components of Articulations and Gradation of Contents (SEP, 2012)

Büşra Yıldız

English Language Curriculum in Ecuador

English Language Education, Bahçeşehir University, Istanbul, Turkey,
busra.yildiz1@bahcesehir.edu.tr

Abstract

Ecuador is a country in northwestern South America and is originally home to various Indigenous Indian tribes. In Ecuador, all educational programs (primary and secondary) are mandated by the Ministry of Education, except for higher education, which is regulated by a national technical council. This chapter introduces the features of the overall education system, and the language teaching system of Ecuador explicitly examines Ecuador's national curriculum by putting emphasis on foreign language education fundamentally and gives relevant recommendations for improvements.

Keywords: Ecuador, English language curriculum, English language teaching, English as a foreign language

Introduction

Ecuador is a country in northwestern South America bordered by Colombia, Peru, and the Pacific Ocean. Its capital city is Quito, and it is originally home to various Indigenous Indian tribes. The country's official language is Spanish; however, the locals continue to use other American dialects. Based on 2019 and 2020 data from UNESCO, the enrollment rate in pre-primary education is 56 % while it is 47.9 % in the tertiary level of education.

Education System in Ecuador

Education System in Ecuador

Education	School/Level	Grades	Age	Years
Primary	Primary School	1–6	6–12	6
Secondary	Secondary Education		12–18	6
Post-secondary	Post-Secondary Education			2
Tertiary	Bachelor's Degree			4
Tertiary	Master's Degree			2
Tertiary	Doctorate			3–6

Figure 1 Education System in Ecuador (Scholaro Database, 2021)

The formal education system of Ecuador comprises four stages which are pre-primary, primary, secondary, and higher education. For children aged 2–6, attendance at a pre-primary school is not required but for children aged 6–14, education is obligatory and free; however, families are responsible for additional costs like fees and transportation. Secondary education is divided into 2 three-year cycles which are the basic cycle and the varied cycle. Further education is possible after the second cycle. Furthermore, depending on the specialization, 4–7 years are spent in university and there are at least 61 universities in Ecuador (Education Encyclopedia, 2021).

In Ecuador, along with the state schools, almost 20 % of elementary and secondary schools are run by private schools. Moreover, all educational programs are mandated by the Ministry of Education, except for higher education, which is regulated by a national technical council. In the Sierra and Costa areas of the country, the school year is traditionally varied. Schools in the Sierra run from October to July, whereas those in the costa run from April or May to December or January. This system, which was built on both climatic and economic factors, has resulted in national coordination issues and a divided regionalism.

In the primary years, examinations are administered at the end of 2 three-year cycles. For secondary education, tests are administered at the conclusion of every cycle. Also, entrance exams for university programs are given. In Ecuador, the education of children in rural areas remains the most problematic issue, and officials are working hard to promote a bilingual school system. Because Spanish is the most widely spoken language in Ecuador, there are numerous Spanish schools. Governments, on the other hand, are eager to popularize the teaching of other languages in the name of development (Education Encyclopedia, 2021).

English Language Education in Ecuador

It is undeniable that English is the most widely spoken language in the world. As a result of globalization, around 25 % of the world's population speaks English in some capacity (Crystal, 2003), and this number is expected to rise. The present government in Ecuador, led by economist Rafael Correa, places a high value on English language learning in order to improve Ecuador's international reputation, and the popular perception of English is favorable because it is linked to wealth and greater employment chances (British Council, 2015).

In Ecuadorian public schools, English is elective until Grade 8, after which it is required. The National English Curriculum mandates English competency targets beginning in Grade 8 and is based on CEFR reference levels: A1 (beginner) in Grades 8–9, A2 (elementary) in Grade 10, and B1 (intermediate) in Grades 11–12. Furthermore, in public schools, 5 hours of English are mandatory after Rafael Correa's regulations.

In Ecuador, there are major inequalities in access to English language instruction. High-income inequality and poverty rates are to blame for this inequality; despite improvements in these measures, socioeconomic status proceeds to constrain access to high-quality private education, along with additional private educational costs and English language instruction. As public schools have fewer assets and competent instructors, as well as tremendous class sizes, the English language instruction quality in those institutions is frequently poor. There also exist territorial disparities in English language training: Agriculture is a key industry in more vulnerable rural areas, and accessing technology is constrained, coming about in less English exposure (British Council, 2015).

National English Curriculum of Ecuador

The Ministry of Education created a new National English Curriculum and mandated English instructors' proficiency in the language. In this light, as part of its overarching objective, which is enabling high-quality public education for everyone, the government has implemented this new national English curriculum and related measures, which have received widespread approval in Ecuador. In order to meet the demands of a linguistically and culturally diverse community and to encourage learners' engagement in education regardless of their L1, this curriculum offers a foundation and framework for learning English as well as embracing authentic, socially pertinent production and activities. Its goal is to help Ecuadorian citizens establish policies that would allow them to effectively communicate in today's globally connected world.

By strengthening intellectual, social, and creative skills in relation to language learning, the curriculum moreover underpins broader educational goals of integrity, creativity, and unity. Students in Ecuador are going to need these skills to succeed in 21st-century societies both locally and internationally. Lastly, by providing learners with exciting and enjoyable learning experiences, this curriculum hopes to instill a love of learning languages in them from an early age, encouraging them to continue learning English in school, at work, and beyond.

When developing the National English Curriculum Guidelines, the Education Ministry drew on the CEFR and Communicative-Functional Language Approach. Upon these guidelines, English became mandatory for five 45-minute to 1-hour courses per week from grade 8 and optional for Grades 2–7. The aim was to raise learners' listening, speaking, reading, and writing skills to a minimum of B1 level.

Furthermore, the Education Ministry has issued guidelines for teachers of English on how to create lesson plans and integrate them into the class, term, and year's learning objectives. The guidelines encourage a communicative strategy and the concept of language as a mechanism for the production and transmission of meaning along with the main tool for interaction and communication.

Sevy-Biloon et al. (2020) state that one crucial factor in ELT that the teachers took into consideration was the infrastructure that is available or not in the public schools where EFL is taught. In their study, many teachers expressed dissatisfaction with the absence of equipment, such as projectors, screens, internet connection, and whiteboards, in addition to having too many students in too few small classrooms. They also added that this made it nearly impossible for them to carry out communicative language teaching CLT implementation activities in pairs and groups.

Considering the operation of the program and teaching-learning processes, specifically lesson design and delivery of Ecuador's mandatory curriculum, in Sevy-Biloon and his colleagues' (2020) study many teachers reported that it was challenging to develop and implement in their classes since they lacked preparation in the pedagogical areas indicated in the curriculum and were not given enough time to do so.

Despite these comments from the teachers, the suggested EFL curriculum emphasizes "learner-centered" learning. It can be concluded that the curriculum in Ecuador particularly is consistent over the country, and the Ministry of Education sets the objectives (rather than instructors or students). Teachers will be expected to do more than simply present cases and knowledge to the public. They will be inspired to recognize that every one of their students is a unique person with a distinctive learning style, identity, and enthusiasm, along with varying levels of capacity and motivation (Nunan, 1988).

The EFL curriculum of Ecuador is also built on a CLIL (Content and Language Integrated Learning) method, in which subjects from different fields of studies are employed for significant and intentional use of language (Met, 1999). Furthermore, the proposed EFL curriculum is communicative in nature, as indicated in the Ministry of Education Documents: Updating and Strengthening the Curriculum 2010.

CLIL	4Cs	Curricular Threads	Sub-Threads
	Culture / Citizenship	Communication and Cultural Awareness	Intercultural Awareness and Identity
			Social Competence and Values
		Oral Communication (Listening and Speaking)	Listening Skills
			Spoken Production
	Communication		Spoken Interaction
		Reading	Literacy-rich Environment
			Reading Comprehension
	Cognition		Use of Resources & Study Skills
			Cross-curricular Content
	Content	Writing	Initial Literacy
			Text Production
		Language through the Arts	Literary Texts in Context
			Creative Writing
			Creative Thinking Skills

Figure 2 CLIL Threads (Ministerio De Educación, 2019)

As Sevy-Biloon et al. (2020) mentioned in their study, many teachers stated that when they attempted to start English clubs or extracurricular activities to encourage English language learning, the administration of their schools did not help them, and then, they were unable to accomplish the activities they had planned.

Furthermore, in terms of assessment issues, the EFL curriculum points out that the nature of assessment is more formative than summative, and it supports frequent feedback to the instructor that can be utilized for developing and enhancing future education. Furthermore, new and varied kinds of evaluation, such as observations, interviews, journals, and portfolios, are necessary to move beyond the restricted assessment of lower-order cognitive abilities so that they can develop a thorough depiction of what students can do in a foreign language.

Conclusion

The government's efforts to boost Ecuador's global competitiveness by enhancing and expanding the chances for Ecuadorians to study abroad have been impressive (Ureña Moreno, 2014). However, more needs to be done, such as re-designing the curriculum so that English instruction begins in the 1st grade and an all-content English class is taught in the 12th grade, raising the English language requirement for secondary school English instructors (grades 9–12) to C1 and creating an institution that is responsible for providing periodic teacher training on techniques to teaching English as a foreign language. Aziz et al. (2018) also point out that more student-centered methodologies must be used to ensure students' mental and physical growth through co-curricular and extracurricular activities.

References

Aziz, S., Mahmood, M., & Rehman, Z. (2018). Implementation of CIPP model for quality evaluation at school level: A case study. *Journal of Education and Educational Development, 5*(1), 189–206.

British Council (2015). *English in Ecuador: An examination of policy, perceptions and influencing factors.* London: Education Intelligence.

Education Encyclopedia (2021) – StateUniversity.com, *Ecuador Educational* System — overview. https://education.stateuniversity.com/pages/400/Ecuador-EDUCATIONAL-SYSTEM-OVERVIEW.html

Met, M. (1999). *Content-based instruction: Defining terms, making decisions.* NFLC Reports. Washington, DC: The National Foreign Language Center.

Ministerio De Educación (2019). *Educación General Básica Currículo de los Niveles de Educación Obligatoria Subnivel Medio.*

Nunan, D. (1988). *The learner-centered curriculum.* Cambridge: Cambridge University Press.

Scholaro Pro. (2021). https://www.scholaro.com/db/Countries/Ecuador/Educat
ion-System.

Sevy-Biloon, J., Recino, U., & Munoz, C. (2020). Factors affecting English language teaching in public schools in Ecuador. *International Journal of Learning,
Teaching and Educational Research, 19*(3), 276–294.

Ureña Moreno, N. E. (2014). *English education in the ecuadorian public
sector: Gaps and recommendations.*

Ayşegül Liman Kaban, PhD.

English Language Curriculum in Israel

*Computer Education and Instructional Technologies, Bahçeşehir University,
Istanbul, Turkey,
aysegul.liman@st.bau.edu.tr*

Abstract

The most important foreign language in Israel is English, which is also widely used in academic papers, in the press, and as a tool in higher education. In Israel, English serves as both a global and a local language in a variety of fields, including business, media, and education, as well as in everyday interactions. English is the language that students are required to read in most academic disciplines; it is frequently peppered in Hebrew oral interactions, particularly among youth in urban areas; it is a language that is widely used in cyberspace and global and high-tech companies, and it is a language that is heard in most films and television programs with translations but no dubbing. Finally, it is a language that all learners must acquire from the beginning of elementary school until the end of secondary school; also, a high level of English is required for admission to higher education institutions.

Keywords: English as a Foreign Language, English teachers, Israel, Curriculum, English Language Teaching

Introduction

Israel is a nation which was established in 1948 because of a declaration of independence that fulfilled the Jewish people's long-held dream of having their own homeland. The president serves as the head of state, which is a parliamentary democracy (Nuffic, 2017). Israel is a nation of immigrants, with citizens hailing from more than 80 different nationalities, which has led to a variety of population groups with a wide range of racial, cultural, and religious roots. Jews make up about 76 % of the population, Arabs (including Muslims and Christians) make up about 20 %, and Druze, Christians, and other ethnicities make up the remaining 4 %.

Socioeconomic status is another important factor, and it has a greater impact on learning outcomes than gender and immigration status in the majority of

Organization for Economic Cooperation and Development (OECD) nations. In Israel, the percentage of kids in the lowest index of economic, social, and cultural status (ESCS) quartile who achieved at least PISA level 2 in reading in 2018 was 43 % lower than that of kids in the highest ESCS quartile, exceeding the OECD average of 29 % by a significant margin. Maintaining a high employment-to-population ratio is essential for economic growth, and the rising participation of women in the workforce has increased with the help of early childhood education and care (ECEC) services. ECEC is important for laying the groundwork for cognitive development and lessening the impact of inequality later in life. Although Israel has one of the highest rates of 3-year-olds enrolled in early childhood education among OECD countries, it has one of the lowest rates of enrollment for students aged 6–14 (OECD, 2021). The length of the military service in Israel – nearly 3 years for men and 2 years for women – affects the comparability of the enrolment rates of young individuals internationally. Most young people in Israel drop out of school between the ages of 18 and 24, which is higher than the average for OECD countries, and this is most probably because of the military service (OECD, 2021). The purpose of this chapter is to explain the education system in Israel and to draw a picture of the English as a Foreign Language environment.

Education System in Israel

In Israel, compulsory education begins at the age of 3. With 47 % of children under two enrolling in ECEC services in 2017, compared to an average of 24 % across OECD nations, the nation also emphasizes the early stages of ECEC. Maintaining a high employment-to-population ratio is essential for economic growth, and the rise in female work has increased interest on the part of the government in increasing ECEC programs. ECEC is important for laying the groundwork for cognitive development and lessening the impact of inequality later in life. The teaching of young children has a long history in Israel. Kindergartens are crucial in fostering a shared identity among children who had immigrated from various nations. In Israel, children must attend school until they are 3 years old since 1984.

According to Nuffic (2017), National legislation that is carried out by the Ministry of Education, Culture, and Sport governs the Israeli educational system. Furthermore, the most significant laws controlling elementary, secondary, and higher education were passed in 1949, 1953, and 1958, respectively. For children from 3 to 15 (until grade 10), public education has been both required and free since 1949. The age for compulsory education is being gradually raised to include students in grades 11 and 12 of secondary school. As is seen in Figure 1, pre-primary, primary, secondary, post-secondary, and higher education make up the five levels of the national education system. There are 3 years of lower-secondary education (grades 7–9), 3 years of upper-secondary education (grades 10–12), and 6 years of primary school (grades 1–6). Academic education and higher professional education are not separated in Israel. Some programs combine components of university education with those from higher professional education. The primary/secondary school year lasts from the end of August through June, while the academic year lasts from October until June. The medium of instruction is either Hebrew or Arabic.

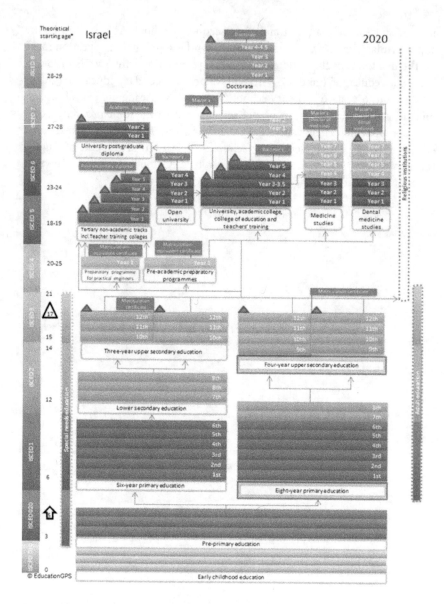

Figure 1 Education System in Israel (OECD, 2021)

In Israel, there are four different kinds of schools, and they can be categorized as primary and secondary education. Part of the curriculum will depend on the type of school; however, all public schools are supported by the Ministry of Education, and they are required to offer the core curriculum as well as subjects that are pertinent to the target audience.

In Israel, primary education starts at the age of 3 years. Primary education consists of a pre-primary (kindergarten) session that is required, followed by 6 years of primary school (until age 12). For the Jewish and Arab communities, elementary education is provided in state schools.

There are 3 years of lower secondary school for the students aged 12–15. Moreover, 3 years of upper secondary school make up secondary education (ages 15–18). The general track and the technical track are the two different pathways that students in upper-secondary education can select from.

Lower secondary education lasts 3 years and consists of general topics like arithmetic, science, English, Hebrew, Arabic, French, geography, social studies, religious studies, and physical education. State-religious schools in Israel give religion two times (as much time as public schools do), while Arab schools teach both Hebrew and Arabic. Students proceed on to one of the two upper-secondary education pathways after finishing grade 9. The outcomes from grades 7 to 9 play a role in determining the type of higher secondary education that students will pursue. After grade 9, no diploma is awarded.

In general, all public sector schools offer two upper secondary education programs (secular state-education schools, state-religious schools, and Arab schools). No matter which track they choose, all students must meet the core curriculum standards, the general requirements of which are established by the Ministry of Education. Nevertheless, depending on students' interests and aptitudes, grades 10–12 offer more room for supplementary and special studies outside of the core curriculum. The amount of time allotted to general and technological courses distinguish the general and technological tracks' curricula most significantly. Both programs get students ready for their final exams as well as for postsecondary admission. The final exam is known as the Bagrut, which measures the knowledge gained during secondary school, is created and graded by the Ministry of Education, and is taken by the majority of students in grade 12. Admission to higher education requires Bagrut.

English Language Curriculum

The Revised English Curriculum 2018 underwent review and redesign, and the result is the English Curriculum 2020. As cited by the Israel Ministry of Education (2020a), the curriculum is evolved from the previous curriculum in many ways and is now in line with worldwide standards to improve the quality of English language education throughout the nation's educational system. The Common European

Framework of Reference for Languages (CEFR) (Council of Europe, 2011, 2018), which is now widely used around the world and defines the competencies necessary for language learners to function and communicate effectively in English, is aligned with the English Curriculum 2020 to address these needs (Israel Ministry of Education, 2020a). Examples of syllabi can be seen in Figures 1 and 2.

UNIT	WRITTEN / SPOKEN RECEPTION		SPOKEN PRODUCTION
1 SUPERHEROES (Page 7)	PART 1 **Meet the Superheroes** Magazine Article PART 2 (Listening) **Who Doesn't Love Superheroes?** Interview PART 3 **Born to Be Special, Born to Save the World** Article PART 4 **I Want to Be …** Poem	• Comparing and contrasting • Predicting • Making connections LITERARY TERMS Poem Stanza Rhymes	Talk about superheroes using new words and expressions Ask and answer questions about why superheroes are popular Express opinions about their favorite superhero story Discuss opinions about a poem Talk about things they want to change in the world Express their wishes about themselves

Figure 2 Syllabus from Be a Hero, 6th Grade Coursebook

WRITTEN PRODUCTION	VOCABULARY and LANGUAGE	TASK
Write descriptions about superheroes Mini Task: Find out about a different superhero and write a short description using the Present Simple	LANGUAGE **Present Simple:** • Positive • Negative • Yes / No questions • WH- questions • Time expressions Prepositions for time expressions: *in, on, at* REVIEW *have / has* *am / is / are* WORD EXPANSION Compound words PUNCTUATION Capital letters	Create new superheroes to help fight sugar

Figure 3 Syllabus from Be a Hero, 6th Grade Coursebook

The English Curriculum 2020 offers a broad framework of reference by outlining explicit, approachable, and achievable propositions that describe the language learners' competencies. It meets the requirements of the Israeli Ministry of Education in terms of the competences, skills, and strategies required within each of the Revised English Curriculum 2018 domains which are Social Interaction; Access to Information; Presentation; and Appreciation of Literature and Culture, and Language. Additionally, it corresponds with contemporary theories on language learning and usage as well as international norms. Table 1 compares the developmental stages identified by the English Curriculum 2020, the CEFR Global Scale, and the Revised English Curriculum 2018.

Table 1 Vocabulary Bands for Each Level (Taken from English Curriculum 2020)

Level	Lexical Band	Grade Level
Pre-Basic User (Pre-A1)	Pre-Band I	Grade 3 and/or first months of Grade 4
Basic User 1 (A1)	Band I Core I Band I Core II	Grade 4 – Mid-Grade 5 Grade 5 – End Grade 6
Basic User 2 (A2)	Band II Core I Band II Core II	Grade 7 – Mid-Grade 8 Grade 8 – End Grade 9
Independent User 1 (B1)	Band III (4 points)	Grade 10 – Grade 12
Independent User 2 (B2)	Band III (5 points)	Grade 10 – Grade 12

Another important factor that must be stressed is that all instructional materials need to be approved by the Ministry of Education. There are some principles to create instructional materials in Israel and all of the instructional materials need to be evaluated by the Ministry of Education. The selection of materials is guided by the following principles.

All instructional materials:

cover the can-do statements (activities and communicative competences), lexical bands and grammar component of the English Curriculum 2020;
are inclusive, unprejudiced, inoffensive and non-stereotypical;
include a variety of text types and media;
are targeted to meet a variety of purposes as well as different audiences;
provide opportunities for action-oriented, contextualized language practice and use;
are appropriate to the age and language proficiency level of the learner;
build on learners' backgrounds, interests, experiences and prior knowledge;
enrich learners' general world knowledge and encourage further exploration;
provide opportunities for meaningful communication;
promote independent and self-regulated learning;
motivate learners to seek out further exposure to the language through reading, listening and viewing (Israel Ministry of Education, 2020a, p. 12)

The design of tasks is also guided by the upcoming principles. All tasks:

are meaningful;
are transparent to the learner in terms of goals, on-going process and product;
focus on form and meaning;
afford opportunities for recycling and enrichment of linguistic and communicative competences;
encourage convergent and divergent thinking;
link to the learners' prior knowledge and experiences;
provide opportunities for applying global competences including critical thinking, problem solving, metacognition, collaboration and creativity;
allow learners to respond using multiple modes of expression (e.g. drawing, writing, singing);
promote opportunities for peer interaction;
provide learners with simulated or real-world issues to apply or adapt new knowledge;
broaden learners' horizons and motivate them to find out about other cultures through creative texts (including literature);
encourage learners to use English as a means for gaining information in other subject areas;
promote learner reflection and self-evaluation (Israel Ministry of Education, 2020a, p. 13).

Figure 4 Sample Grammar Explanation from 6th-Grade Coursebook

Local MoE-approved coursebooks often include reading passages, poems, stories, and exercises after each. Each unit has resources for a variety of learning tasks, including dictation, pronunciation, recitation, role-playing, reading, writing, drama, drawing, and role-playing. Examples of activities can be analyzed in Figures 2 to 5.

READ   **E**   1. **Before you read, find FIVE of the new words. Check if you understand the sentences they are in.**

2. **Read about four superheroes and learn about their special powers.**

Meet the Superheroes

1

Wonder Woman is a famous superhero. Her real name is Diana Prince. Her mother is the queen of the Amazons. Wonder Woman has many special powers. She is very strong. She can run and fly very fast. And she never dies! Wonder Woman usually saves people. She has black hair. She wears special clothes. She has a blue skirt and red boots.

TRUE or FALSE?

1. Wonder Woman can run and fly very fast.
2. Wonder Woman is the queen of the Amazons.
3. Wonder Woman never dies.
4. Wonder Woman has a red skirt and black boots.

2

Superman is a famous superhero too. He comes from Planet Krypton[1]. His real name is Kal-El. His parents send him to Earth to save his life. On Earth, he has a new name, Clark Kent. Superman is very strong, and he can run and fly very fast. Superman always saves people with his special powers. His clothes are blue and red with the letter "S" on them.

1. Why do Superman's parents send him to Earth?
2. Write TWO special powers Superman has.
3. Where does Superman come from?
4. What is Superman's real name?

1. Planet Krypton   כוכב הלכת קריפטון / كوكب كريبتون

10

Figure 5 Sample Reading Activity for 6th-Grade Coursebook

It is a requirement for all Israeli children to study two foreign languages. However, the majority of elementary schools start teaching it in the 3rd grade, while others start in the first or second. All pupils are required to learn English until they graduate from the 4th grade (Israel Ministry of Education, 2020b). All academic institutions demand a passing score on the English matriculation exam as well as the English for Academic Purposes (EAP) entrance exam as a requirement for admission, and it is the first foreign language taught in the entire educational system (Carmel & Badash, 2019). Due to the growing popularity of the English language in Israel, there is a greater demand for English study and a lower beginning age for English instruction in schools, creating a significant need for proficient, high-quality English teachers throughout the entire country (Vysvalai, 2017 as cited in (Carmel & Badash, 2019).

Conclusion

In this chapter, the researcher examined Israel and the English curriculum's structure. The English language nowadays is defined as being strategically situated at a crossroads in the context of Israel's diversified and complicated cultural reality. It is undeniably present and is quickly expanding in the social, cultural, and economic life of the nation. The number of people who become proficient in the language increases every year, especially among younger age groups. This gives better prospects in the market that is getting more competitive.

References

Carmel, R., & Badash, M. (2019). Who is the effective teacher? Perceptions of early career English teachers in Israel. *The Language Learning Journal, 49*(5), 614–629. doi: 10.1080/09571736.2019.1656767

Council of Europe (2011). Common European Framework of Reference for Languages: Learning, Teaching, Assessment. Council of Europe. https://www.coe.int/en/web/language-policy/home?e1_en.asp

Council of Europe (2018). Common European Framework of Reference for Languages: Learning, Teaching, Assessment. Companion Volume with New Descriptors. Council of Europe. https://rm.coe.int/cefr-companion-volume-with-new-descriptors2018/1680787989

Israel Ministry of Education (2020a). English Curriculum 2020 For Elementary School. Pedagogical Secretariat, Ministry of Education. https://meyda.education.gov.il/files/Mazkirut_Pedagogit/English/curriculum2020Elementary.pdf

Israel Ministry of Education (2020b). Bulletin of the Chief inspectors for English. http://cms.education.gov.il/EducationCMS/Units/Mazkirut_Pedagogit/English/InspectoratesDesk/HozerMafmar.htm. Crossref.

Nuffic (2017). Education System in Israel. https://www.nuffic.nl/en/education-systems/israel

OECD (2021). Education at a Glance 2021: OECD Indicators. OECD Publishing, Paris, https://doi.org/10.1787/b35a14e5-en.

About the Editor

Nihal Yurtseven, Ph.D., is an associate professor at the Department of Educational Sciences, Bahçeşehir University, Istanbul, Turkey. She received her Ph.D. degree in curriculum and instruction with a specialization in instructional design at Yildiz Technical University, Istanbul, Turkey. So far, she has researched about instructional design, teachers' professional development, the relationship between teachers' professional development and students' achievement, and numerous variables affecting student learning. Specifically, she has carried out several experimental, mixed method, and action research studies to understand the impact of instructional interventions on the learning process. In addition, she has organized seminars and workshops about the integration of instructional design models into diverse disciplines at various educational institutions, and she has presented her studies at different conferences. Teacher education, instructional design, mentorship, teamwork, professional learning communities, peer coaching, and individual differences are among her fields of interest. She has various scientific studies, book chapters, and national/international presentations about these fields. She also has been teaching courses in the field of educational sciences at the graduate and undergraduate levels. She is currently the coordinator of a national project, named Designer Teacher. She is also the current director of Center for Learning and Teaching (CLT) in Bahçeşehir University. E-mail: nihal.yurtseven@es.bau.edu.tr

About the Authors

Sezgin Ballıdağ is a language instructor at Yıldız Technical University, School of Foreign Languages, and Ph.D. candidate at English Language Teaching department at Bahçeşehir University. He earned his MA degree in ELT from Kocaeli University and BA degree from Hacettepe University. Besides teaching English, he has also worked as a Turkish instructor at the University of Richmond, VA, the USA as a Fulbright Scholar. His research interests include testing and assessment, online assessment, assessment literacy, and bilingual education.
E-mail: sezgin.ballidag@bahcesehir.edu.tr

Nurhan Çökmez, is an instructor who has been teaching English as a foreign language for 10 years. Currently, she is a Ph.D. student in ELT at Bahcesehir University.
e-mail: nurhan.cokmez@bahcesehir.edu.tr

Rabia Dinçer, Ph.D. student in Bahçeşehir University, ELT program, is an English language instructor at National Defence University. Her research interests are educational technologies, curriculum development, bilingualism, and positive psychology in SLA.
E-mail: rabia.gungor@bahcesehir.edu.tr

Kevser Kaya is a Ph.D. student at the department of English Language Teaching (ELT) of Bahçeşehir University, İstanbul, Turkey. She is an English instructor in the school of foreign languages, at Harran University, Şanlıurfa, Turkey. She has been working for 12 years now. Her research interests are teacher education, teacher professional development, and curriculum development.
Email: kevser.kaya1@bahcesehir.edu.tr

Tuğçe Kılıç (MA in ELT) is a lecturer at Istanbul University – Cerrahpasa School of Foreign Languages and a Ph.D. student in ELT department of Bahcesehir University, Istanbul. Her research is on CALL, teacher identity, and curriculum design.
E-mail: tugce.kilic@bahcesehir.edu.tr

Tuba Kıvanç Contuk is a Ph.D. student at Bahçeşehir University. After 10 years of experience in teaching English as a foreign language, she currently works as a deputy headmaster at a state school. She has conducted many Erasmus+ projects as well as given consultancy to teachers about the application and implementation process in the district directorate of national education. Her research

interests include second language acquisition in young learners and multilingualism with a specific focus on trilingualism.
E-mail: tuba.kivanccontuk@bahcesehir.edu.tr

Ayşegül Liman Kaban is an assistant professor at Bahcesehir University, Computer Education and Instructional Technologies Department. Her research interests include digital pedagogy, gamification in education, distance education, blended learning, and online collaborative learning.
Email: aysegul.liman@sfl.bau.edu.tr

Merve Nur Özet has completed her MA at Hacettepe University. She has worked as an English instructor in preparatory classes at various universities, and she still is an English instructor at TOBB Economy and Technology university. Her extensive experience in teaching English to adult learners helps her define her research interests as teaching pragmatics and pragmatic competence.
E-mail: mervenur.ozet@bahcesehir.edu.tr

Büşra Yıldız, Ph.D. student in Bahçeşehir University English Language Teaching (ELT) program, is an English language instructor at Yıldız Technical University School of Foreign Languages. Her research interests are technology in education, teacher education in educational technology, curriculum development, and bilingual education.
E-mail: busra.yildiz1@bahcesehir.edu.tr

Rumeysa Yücel, Ph.D. student in Bahcesehir University ELT program, is an English Language instructor at Turkish Air Force Academy, National Defence University. Her research interests are ESP curriculum development, teacher education in educational technology, and bilingual education.
E-mail: rumeysa.yucel@bahcesehir.edu.tr

www.ingramcontent.com/pod-product-compliance
Lightning Source LLC
LaVergne TN
LVHW050143060326
832904LV00004B/143